E. T. A. Hoffmann's Other World

THE ROMANTIC AUTHOR AND
HIS "NEW MYTHOLOGY"

University of Pennsylvania Studies
in Germanic Languages and Literatures

Edited by

ANDRE VON GRONICKA : OTTO SPRINGER

With the cooperation of

Adolph C. Gorr
Adolph D. Klarmann
Albert L. Lloyd
Heinz Moenkemeyer
Alfred Senn

E. T. A. Hoffmann's *Other World*

THE ROMANTIC AUTHOR AND HIS "NEW MYTHOLOGY"

by Kenneth Negus

Philadelphia
University of Pennsylvania Press

833.6
N31e

5 6040
Nov.'66

To My Wife

Preface

This book treats a single phase of Hoffmann's literary accomplishment, his "new mythology," without attempting a complete coverage of his total artistic production or general significance. This limited approach is such, however, that an examination of all of his major literary works and most of the minor ones was necessary; and they are discussed here, I believe, with the emphasis that is proper for their overall merits. Furthermore, several assessments in the monograph will undoubtedly suggest much of Hoffmann's importance in German Romanticism, and as an author of imaginative tales that occupy a unique and influential place in the history of nineteenth-century European literature.

The beginnings of my interest in Hoffmann go back more than ten years. Since then many of my former teachers and colleagues have given me considerable assistance and encouragement in the Hoffmann studies leading to this one. I wish to express here special appreciation to Professor Walter Silz of Columbia University, under whose instruction at Princeton I first read the German Romanticists; to Professor Bernhard Ulmer of Princeton University, who patiently supervised my first attempt to establish some basic principles of Hoffmann's narrative technique; and to my German colleagues, Dr. Friedrich Schnapp of Hamburg and Dr. Wolfgang Kron of the University of Munich, for their help and good will in several phases of my research on Hoffmann. I wish also to thank Professor Johannes Nabholz of Rutgers University for constant interest in my book during the past few years, and for helpful suggestions; to Professor Stuart Atkins of Harvard University for his interest; to the editors of the *Germanic Review,* who permitted me to reprint in Chapter II parts of an article that had appeared in their journal; to the Research Council of Rutgers University for generous support during the writing and final preparation of the manuscript; and to Professors André von Gronicka and Heinz Moenkemeyer of the University of Pennsylvania for valuable editorial counsel.

New Brunswick, N. J.   Kenneth Negus
March, 1964

Contents

E. T. A. Hoffmann's Other World

THE ROMANTIC AUTHOR AND
HIS "NEW MYTHOLOGY"

1

Introduction

E. T. A. Hoffmann's tales present an unusual challenge to
the serious student of literature. As the pre-eminent writer
of fantasy, he charms and amuses, but also bewilders his
reader with an apparent overabundance of pure inventiveness. His writings may seem to offer little more than a delightful game of the imagination. Extended neglect of
him by German literary scholars seemed to lend support
to this reaction in the past, for in his native land Hoffmann was regarded mainly as a mere literary entertainer
throughout most of the nineteenth century. That his
works deserved more serious attention, is strongly suggested by their overwhelming influence on such writers
outside Germany as Dostoevski, Baudelaire, and Edgar
Allan Poe, who held him in highest esteem.

Furthermore, a legend about Hoffmann, the man, arose
and tended to obscure his works. It told of an unfortunate
creature afflicted with a sordid kind of alcoholism, tortured

Byronism, and immorality. Although there is some truth to this image of Hoffmann, it has often conveyed exaggerations and irrelevancies to his readers, giving rise, for example, to the grossly distorted "Hoffmann" of Offenbach's opera. Fortunately, considerable progress has been made by critics and scholars of this century in dispelling misconceptions, and in penetrating more deeply into his unique artistry.

The aim of this book is to examine his whole literary career and production in order to establish part of a valid and useful critical foundation for his narrative art. I see this mainly in a special type of Romantic mythology that was developed in theory and practice by the major authors of his generation.

Early in the Romantic movement (1800), the "new mythology" was formulated succinctly in Friedrich Schlegel's programmatic dictum in the essay, "Rede über die Mythologie" in *Gespräch über die Poesie*. He contends here that the literary art of his time lacked a "Mittelpunkt" such as that provided by mythology in ancient Greece and Rome. He claimed that a *new* mythology was needed—one that would differ from that of the Ancients in that it would *not* consist of the materials of the familiar, sensual world about us, but would be formed ". . . aus der tiefsten Tiefe des Geistes . . . es muss das künstlichste aller Kunstwerke seyn, denn es soll alle andern erfassen, ein neues Bette und Gefäss für den alten ewigen Urquell der Poesie und selbst das unendliche Gedicht, welches die Keime aller andern Gedichte verhüllt."[1]

It is assumed that the immediate environment of Schlegel's times could not be the ultimate source of the poetic. This is a fundamental idea of "Brief über den

[1] Friedrich Schlegel, *Seine prosaischen Jugendschriften*, ed. J. Minor (Wien, 1882), II, 358.

Roman," also in *Gespräch über die Poesie*; it is also
indicated explicitly in "Rede über die Mythologie": "Aus
dem Innern herausarbeiten, das alles muss der moderne
Dichter. . . ."[2] Literature had thus to be nourished from a
profound and invisible area of the human mind. This
poetic source is "ancient," yet is also "eternal," and therefore must exist somewhere at all times—although, we may
add, it may not always be immediately accessible. Thus
the "Ur-" prefix in "Urquell" gives us the double concept
of *ancient* and *original*, of primeval and primal.

This does not mean, however, that *only* the writer's
innermost soul was to provide the materials for his works.
On the contrary, this was to be a *cosmic* poetry, described
by Schlegel two years before in the famous "Athenäumsfragment" as "Progressive Universalpoesie": "Sie umfasst
alles, was nur poetisch ist, vom grössten, wieder mehrere
Systeme in sich enthaltenden Systeme der Kunst, bis zu
dem Seufzer, dem Kuss, den das dichtende Kind aushaucht
in kunstlosen Gesang."[3] It is a dynamically progressive
form of literature, always "im Werden," for this Romantic type of poetry alone is infinite, it alone can em-
brace all that the poet may encounter.

Schlegel's "new mythology" is an outgrowth of his
"Progressive Universalpoesie," for in the *Rede über die
Mythologie,* he indicates several possible sources and
analogous cases as first principles and guides for the mythology nourishing this new kind of poetry. German Idealism heads the list. As presented here, it is largely a
subjective idealism, for Schlegel's point of departure—
"the deepest depths of the spirit"—suggests an inward
idea as the source, although at certain points the poetic

---

[2] *Ibid.*
[3] Friedrich Schlegel, *Schriften und Fragmente*, ed. E. Behler (Stuttgart,
1956), p. 93.

object itself, as in the "Athenäumsfragment," initiates the process. Moreover, the new mythology, once accomplished, is to foster a "new, boundless realism," embodying a "harmony of the ideal and the real." Thus his idealistic "new mythology" was to end up, one might say, as a realistic "Progressive Universalpoesie."

Spinoza's writings suggested to Schlegel a further philosophical foundation for Romantic fantasy, grounded in an immanent natural Godhead: ". . . ein klarer Duft schwebt unsichtbar sichtbar über dem Ganzen . . . Und ist nicht dieser milde Widerschein der Gottheit im Menschen die eigentliche Seele, der zündende Funke aller Poesie?"[4] This points to the wider frame of reference of "Progressive Universalpoesie" and "neue Mythologie": Schlegel's efforts ultimately to create a new gospel, embracing a religious, philosophical, cultural, and artistic unity for Western culture. The almost complete failure of Schlegel and his contemporaries to accomplish anything resembling this is, as will be seen, one of the limiting factors in Hoffmann's mythology.

Nonetheless, some of Schlegel's formulations in *Rede über die Mythologie* clearly anticipated Hoffmann's fanciful mythology: "Und was ist jede schöne Mythologie anders als ein hieroglyphischer Ausdruck der umgebenden Natur in dieser Verklärung von Phantasie und Liebe. . . . Was sonst das Bewusstsein ewig flieht, ist hier dennoch sinnlich geistig zu schauen und festgehalten, wie die Seele in dem umgebenden Leibe, durch den sie in unser Auge schimmert, zu unserem Ohre spricht."[5] The concrete-sensual nature of Hoffmann's mythical figures is thus anticipated.

Toward the end of the essay, Schlegel mentions other

[4] *Ibid.*, p. 125.
[5] *Ibid.*, p. 126.

examples of Romantic mythologies. In the works of Shakespeare and Cervantes he sees an "indirect mythology" possessing the qualities of a primal poetic fancy. These two authors, Schlegel claims, created literary arabesques full of wit ("Witz"), fusing things otherwise incompatible with one another. The laws of reason are dissolved, and we experience in their art "die schöne Verwirrung der Phantasie . . . das ursprüngliche Chaos der menschlichen Natur."[6] Nothing Schlegel said is more applicable than this to Hoffmann's bizarre mythical fantasies.

Schlegel emphasizes the endless variety of materials for Romantic mythology and demonstrates how, for example, the new mythology might be enriched by the literatures of the Orient, especially of India. His intense preoccupation with Indian literature and philosophy had not yet begun; thus he referred only to "das höchste Romantische" to be derived from Eastern myths. He might just as well have cited the American Indians, since the point of the paragraph lies in its proposal to use *all* available sources; for myth is potentially universal, and writing myth is a "divination" out of a universal, immanent power.

It is, therefore, erroneous to point to specific sources of Romantic myths as ultimate explanations of their meaning, although such sources may be revealing for individual facets of a given myth. Above all, Schlegel's "new mythology" should not be interpreted as an eclecticism of all available mythical materials, but rather as a product of the creative fantasy of the writer, who is to form his myths with inborn mythogenic faculties, using any materials he encounters—whatever their sources—as poetic figures. In short, the Romantic poet is a *visionary* poet. His mind creates the mold; anywhere might be found the clay. Thus, as will be seen in the course of this monograph,

[6] *Ibid.,* p. 127

the proper point of departure for contemplating Hoffmann's myths is his "idea"—infused into a poetic vision—
of higher, lower, and intermediary cosmic realms, and of
their interaction. This forms the basis for his mythology,
which is presented in concentrated form in *Der goldne
Topf*, and is evident in all other works written by him. To
be sure, Hoffmann utilized many "sources" for his myths;
but without primary reference to the one "ancient, eternal,
original source" of myth in its fundamental visionary
"idea," any other sources provide little more than a
peripheral understanding of its meaning.

In spite of the clear relationship of Schlegel's theory to
Hoffmann's practice, certain discrepancies between them
must be stressed from the start. Above all, it should be
noted that Schlegel's whole project of a single new mythology for his and subsequent generations was an almost
total failure. He and his fellow Romanticists succeeded
only in creating a few personal mythologies, and in resur-
recting fragments of myths from distant lands and times,
which in turn were taken up fragmentarily as myth by
future writers. The new mythology was to become a part
of the very foundation of his culture, and had to be accepted and cultivated by Western Europe as a whole.
Obviously, no such thing came about, not even within the
short span of German Romanticism. Even Schlegel himself later became estranged from much of his literary
theory of the Jena and Berlin phases of early German
Romanticism, including even his "Progressive Universalpoesie";[7] and his emphasis on myth was greatly reduced
in favor of symbolism.[8]

[7] Ernst Behler, "Friedrich Schlegels Theorie der Universalpoesie,"
Jahrbuch der deutschen Schiller-Gesellschaft, I (1947), 211-252.
[8] Liselotte Dieckmann, "Friedrich Schlegel and Romantic Concepts of the
Symbol," *Germanic Review*, XXXIV (1959), 276-283.

Nonetheless this preoccupation with new mythology evoked a wealth of mythical fragments that were woven into coherent, but individual mythologies by most German Romanticists. Among these materials would be included the motifs, figures, and symbolic actions derived from folklore (fairy tales and folk songs), the Orient, the mythologized past (Middle Ages and Sixteenth-Century Germany), Nordic mythology, and, of course, many tropes from classical antiquity and the Judaeo-Christian tradition.[9] A unity—even a unified selection—out of this bewildering assortment could be made and formed into a coherent mythology only on an individual basis. Thus we have a considerable variety of mythical works among the major products of Romanticism, as in the *Kunstmärchen* of Novalis, Tieck, and Brentano; in many of the folksong-like poems of Brentano, Eichendorff, and Heine; and most of all in the various kinds of fantastic tales by Hoffmann.

The profound and invisible "Mittelpunkt," the "Urquell der Poesie" was thus found and made productive in the form of myth, but not according to Schlegel's plan, for as the history of Romantic literature evolved, each new myth was short-lived. The dynamic, protean forces at work in Romanticism, and the lack of generally accepted fundamentals, made it impossible to create a genuine German or West European Olympus. Even Hoffmann's new mythology, coherent as it was in its visionary inception, underwent considerable transformation, and proved to be no more than a provisional mythology.

[9] See Fritz Strich's *Die Mythologie in der deutschen Literatur* (Halle a. d. Saale, 1910) for a detailed treatment of the great variety of myths in this period.

Schlegel's programmatic dictum on Romantic mythology is applicable here only as a point of departure, with many different possible goals and outgrowths. In general, the most important divergence from him is the loss of the greater frames of reference surrounding the concept: that is, the theology and broad cultural philosophy of which it is a product. Emphasis tended to shift from the universal and cosmopolitan to the personal. The poet became more and more the supreme master of his private universe, and could even treat it with profound irony—as Hoffmann almost always did. Such a mythology bears the seeds of its own destruction.

II

Schlegel's proposals for a new mythology had rich possibilities of development, and there are some further facets of the concept revealed in critical statements made by other Romanticists. The outstanding ones having special relevance for Hoffmann are those made by Schelling and Novalis.

Schelling was Hoffmann's favorite Romantic philosopher. We know that he read *Ideen zu einer Philosophie der Natur* and *Von der Weltseele*.[10] Schelling made the important distinction between historical myth (a primitive form of history, conceived actually to have happened), and the philosophical myth, which is not historically true, but pictorializes invisible truths of nature. Hoffmann's myths are of the latter kind, and his visionary mythical

---

[10] See Felix Hasselberg's list of the works which Hoffmann is known to have read in: E. T. A. Hoffmann, *Werke*, ed. Georg Ellinger, 2nd ed. (Leipzig-Berlin, n. d. [1927]), Vol. XV. References to Hoffmann's works will henceforth be to this edition, and will be indicated simply by volume and page number.

creations reflect fundamental natural laws. Schlegel's new mythology was, to be sure, conceived as "ein hieroglyphischer Ausdruck der umgebenden Natur." Schelling, however, developed a whole philosophy centered on an immanent, creative soul in nature. Hoffmann was well aware of this aspect of his own myths, and repeatedly mentioned it—the *locus classicus* being the final sentence of *Der goldne Topf*, in which the author speaks of "das Leben in der Poesie, der sich der heilige Einklang aller Wesen als tiefstes Geheimnis der Natur offenbaret. . . ."

Novalis too enriched the idea of Romantic mythology. Although he did not use the word "Mythologie" very often, his numerous pronouncements on the *Märchen* (the genre in which Hoffmann wrote most of his myths) reveal some of the major aspects of Hoffmann's mythology.[11] "Die Welt des Märchens ist die durchaus entgegengesetzte Welt der Welt der Wahrheit (Geschichte)— und eben darum ihr so durchaus ähnlich, wie das Chaos der vollendeten Schöpfung . . ."; ". . . Bekenntnisse eines wahrhaften, synthetischen Kindes . . ."; "Das Märchen ist gleichsam der Kanon der Poesie—alles Poetische muss märchenhaft sein . . ."; "Das Märchen ist ganz musikalisch. . . ."[12]—such statements that Novalis made in connection with this genre provide, as will be seen, some of the basic

[11] For the relationship of *Märchen* to myth see O. F. Bollnow, *Unruhe und Geborgenheit* (Stuttgart, 1953), p. 194 f.: "Das Spielende am Märchen wird . . . zum Zeichen der Ehrfurcht vor der Sache, der man sich nicht mehr in der plumpen Vertraulichkeit des direkten Zugriffs zu nähern wagt. So wird das Märchen bei Novalis mehr als ein blosses Märchen. Es steigt auf zur Würde des Mythos, wenn auch in dem freieren Sinn, in dem Novalis überhaupt von Mythos spricht: 'Mythologie hier in meinem Sinn, als freie poetische Erfindung, die die Wirklichkeit sehr mannigfach symbolisiert' . . . Die Dichtung wird zum Märchen und das Märchen zum Mythos. . . ."
[12] Novalis, *Werke/Briefe. Dokumente* (Heidelberg, 1957), 2. Band/Fragmente I, Nr. 1460 (the first two quotations), 1464 and 1468.

theoretical assumptions of Hoffmann's mythical *Kunst-märchen.*

In close juxtaposition with Novalis' concept of the *Märchen* stands that of the *Urzeit*, or *Vorzeit* as he terms it. He wrote, for example: "Mit der Zeit muss die Geschichte Märchen werden—sie wird wieder, wie sie anfing."[13] This concept is of utmost importance, for Hoffmann's myths are all of the *Urzeit*—even though they also play a role in modern times. In fact, part of the poet's mission is to realize the *Urzeit* in his own experience through poetry. Thus Schlegel's term "Urquell" takes on fuller meaning.

Novalis' statements do not merely reflect the same *Zeitgeist* which pervades Hoffmann's works, but in all likelihood are more or less direct sources, for we know that Hoffmann read everything by Novalis available at the time.[14] Also, Hoffmann's most avid reading of this poet came toward the end of the Bamberg period (1808-1813), immediately before the writing of *Der goldne Topf.*

Many more Romanticists could be cited to show the great extent to which ideas of a new mythology and closely related topics were widely discussed among Hoffmann's contemporaries. To trace them all would be an extremely complex process. In some cases it would be impossible, since much was obviously conveyed through conversation, or was so much a part of a ubiquitous Romantic *Zeitgeist*, that attempts to point out specific precedents would be misleading.

As for the sources in the literary works of other Ro-

---

13 *Ibid.* no. 1460. Also see *Sehnsucht nach dem Tode* (I, 412 f.): "O! einsam steht und tiefbetrübt, / Wer heiss und fromm die Vorzeit liebt . . . Wir müssen nach der Heimat gehn, / Um diese heilge Zeit zu sehn"); *Heinrich von Ofterdingen* (I, 102 f.); and *Die Lehrlinge zu Sais* (I, 271 f.).
14 See Hasselberg, under "Novalis."

manticists, we encounter a situation in which misinterpre-
tation is a constant danger. The visionary nature of
Romantic mythology makes the relevance of such sources
extremely limited. There can be no doubt that Novalis'
Märchen myths in *Heinrich von Ofterdingen* and *Die
Lehrlinge zu Sais,* and Tieck's demonic *Kunstmärchen*
contributed some specific features to Hoffmann's myths.
Once, however, the literary "dictionary meanings" of certain stock figures and motifs—such as the elemental spirits,
the *vates,* the witch, flowers, stones, metals, etc.—are
established, we must turn to their functions within the
particular myth in which they are found to understand
them fully. It will be shown that the essential structure
and development of Hoffmann's mythology can be found
only in his works—a fact which manifests both the weak-
ness and the strength of a "new mythology," for it must
be learned while reading it, since it is not common
knowledge, as was the mythology of the Ancients. On the
other hand, it raises the author's individuality to cosmic
proportions, in that his personal world-image is central
and all-embracing in the work. It becomes the writer's
prerogative to create his own myth, which the reader may
or may not recognize for what it is. Its existence is indisputable, but it must be identified and interpreted in its
relation to the whole work for the reader not schooled in
this type of mythology, nor in the unique aspects of an
individual writer's mythology.

III

Hoffmann's reputation has experienced uncommonly
severe fluctuations, thus making a truly informed and
critical evaluation of his literary art difficult. Once he
ceased to be regarded as an *Unterhaltungsdichter* around

the turn of the twentieth century, serious scholarship on him was first devoted primarily to biography and inordinately biographical interpretations of his works. The impetus was provided by Georg Ellinger's *E. T. A. Hoffmann. Sein Leben und seine Werke* (1894). The first scholarly edition of Hoffmann's works was then published by Grisebach (1900). Thereupon followed the work of Hans von Müller, the most productive and accomplished of all Hoffmann scholars. It was von Müller who uncovered Hoffmann's hitherto unpublished letters, along with other biographical documents, and edited and published them. His edition of Hoffmann's correspondence with all its "Apparat" remains the most valuable single publication on Hoffmann's life.[15] Meanwhile two excellent scholarly editions of Hoffmann's works were being prepared by Carl Georg von Maassen (1908-1928) and Georg Ellinger (1912).

Von Müller also did considerable editing of Hoffmann's works, providing much valuable commentary. He did not sum up, however, the results of his huge labors on Hoffmann in any single publication. Hoffmann's versatility and productivity made it nearly impossible for one man to write such a comprehensive work at that time. Von Müller's one publication that is in any sense a summation is *Das künstlerische Schaffen E. T. A. Hoffmanns in Umrissen angedeutet* (Leipzig, 1926). I am indebted to it for the idea of dividing Hoffmann's total literary accomplishment into three phases: the artistic, the demonic, and the fantastic ("das Märchenhafte").

---

15 *E. T. A. Hoffmann im persönlichen und brieflichen Verkehr. Sein Briefwechsel und die Erinnerungen seiner Bekannten,* ed. von Müller (Berlin, 1912), cited henceforth as *Briefwechsel*. At the time of this writing, Friedrich Schnapp's revised and expanded edition has not yet been published.

In the midst of Hans von Müller's early works, there appeared a book which stood alone at that time as a highly competent, purely literary treatment of Hoffmann's writings: Paul Sucher's *Les Sources du Merveilleux chez E. T. A. Hoffmann* (Paris, 1912). Since it is a source study, it differs radically in approach from mine. It is still, however, the best book on the subject, and the reader is referred to it particularly for the sources of Hoffmann's mythical motifs, as well as for a discussion of his whole "other world" in the light of his predecessors. The most relevant section is "Le monde des mythes," in which the author properly centers his attention on *Der goldne Topf, Meister Floh,* and *Prinzessin Brambilla.* Sucher does not apply Schlegel's idea of myth here, but develops an eclectic concept derived mainly from Novalis and Schubert.

Hans von Müller strongly influenced those who followed him in his biographical approach. Richard von Schaukal's excellent book, *E. T. A. Hoffmann* (1923), demonstrates this in its sub-title: *Sein Werk aus seinem Leben.* He also repeatedly expresses great indebtedness to von Müller. A writer himself, von Schaukal was among the most perceptive and articulate critics of Hoffmann's works. The biographical sections of the book have far less to offer than the precise and eloquent statements on the tales. He was among the few literary critics at this time to perceive the mythical nature of Hoffmann's *Märchen:* ". . . die Welt des Irdischen ist eingebaut in eine weitere, die sich in Raum- und Zeitlosigkeit verliert. . . . Der dazu berufene Mensch erlebt diese Wirklichkeit als Gegenwart, während seine nächste Umgebung daran nicht teilhat. Es ist der Mythos, die Spiegelung des menschlichen Erlebens im Über- und Unterirdischen, der 'Sinn' des Zufälligen." (p. 269) In his discussions of the *Märchen* themselves, von Schaukal did not devote much further attention to the myth, which he describes here so well.

Walther Harich's book, *E. T. A. Hoffmann: Das Leben eines Künstlers* (1920) shows the same biographical trend in his interpretations as von Schaukal's. It is, however, overburdened to an extreme by plot summaries. While there are a few paragraphs of worthwhile criticism among these summaries and biography, this book has, in this writer's judgment, received far too much attention by scholars and critics, at the expense of Richard von Schaukal's honest and diligent work appearing at about the same time. Although the sub-title would indicate an "artistic" trend in the book, there is little to justify this. It is, in fact, impossible to sum up Harich's approach: the book lacks a Conclusion at the end, and conclusiveness throughout.

After Harich's book, there were no comprehensive works of criticism on Hoffmann throughout the twenties and into the late thirties. There appeared, however, two works of lesser scope which deserve some attention here: those by Egli and Dahmen.

Gustav Egli's *E. T. A. Hoffmann. Ewigkeit und Endlichkeit in seinem Werk* (Zürich/Leipzig/Berlin, 1927) does not concentrate on Hoffmann's myths, but presents a philosophical foundation, derived mainly from Schelling, for some major aspects of his mythology. Hoffmann's Romantic dualistic philosophy emerges here with consummate clarity. Its opposite poles are eternity and finiteness. In this double world Hoffmann's main characters are in a situation described as follows:

> So schafft Hoffmann seine überragend Begnadeten—Gestalten, in denen Pflicht und Trieb, Ewigkeit und Natur, Gott und Mensch sich die Hand gereicht. Sie umgibt er zärtlich mit

der ganzen Schwermut, der seine eigene, kindlich weiche, am Leben unendlich leidende Seele fähig ist; ihnen schenkt er aber auch das Heldentum, das in seinem kleinen, von Schauern der Ewigkeit geschüttelten und ausgeglühten Künstlerkörper brennt, und das den Tod nicht im dunkeln, selbstvergessenen Rausche will, sondern das Leben mit heroischer Gebärde trotz all seiner Verlorenheit als ein von kosmischen Mächten gewolltes erträgt, bis die flüchtige Welle der Zeitlichkeit es ans Ufer des Ewigen hinüberspült (p. 8 f.)

Although the heroism of Hoffmann's main characters seems overstated here, the structure of the basic human situation is accurately described from our present point of view, if one interprets the world of eternity as also that of myth. Hoffmann's mythology does indeed exist in a timeless world, always accessible to those gifted ones—mainly artists—who turn to it. Egli devoted primary attention to *Der goldne Topf* as the fullest expression of the dualistic world-view. Therefore it has the most fully developed myth, as will be seen. Other mythical works which he discusses in detail as supplementary to *Der goldne Topf* are *Klein Zaches* and *Prinzessin Brambilla*. I add only *Meister Floh* to this list as being of major importance. I further agree with Egli in the generally dynamic nature of the mythical world, in which a fundamental creative urge brings about a progressive, infinitely varied multiplication of all creatures and things in it.[16]

Hans Dahmen's *E. T. A. Hoffmanns Weltanschauung* (Marburg, 1929) offers mainly a useful supplement to Sucher's source studies. The bulk of the book is a sensitive

[16] See Karl Ochsner, *E. T. A. Hoffmann als Dichter des Unbewussten* (Frauenfeld/Leipzig, 1936), for an extension of Egli's approach into psychological areas. Here the subconscious mind becomes the faculty for entering the mythical world of eternity. Ochsner explicitly states his close dependence on Egli (pp. 16-20).

discussion of correspondences between passages in Hoffmann's works, and those of Schubert, Novalis, Tieck,
Fouqué, Reil, Villars, and Gozzi. The study tends to cor-
roborate my assumption that *Der goldne Topf* is the
proper point of departure for an approach to Hoffmann's
myths, for Dahmen states in his introduction: "Im Mittelpunkt der Untersuchung steht Hoffmanns Märchen 'Der
goldne Topf'; denn dies ist sein bestes Werk, von dem aus
alles Vorherige und Nachfolgende gedeutet werden kann.
. . ." (p. 2) The sum total of the study is not, however,
what its misleading title suggests. Dahmen's perspicacious
source-seeking, with all its detail, absorbs much attention
away from *Weltanschauung*, so that only in isolated passages do comprehensive views of Hoffmann's world emerge.
One such point is of some interest here: where he discusses the problem of Hoffmann's apparent simultaneous
belief and disbelief in the mythical world. "Eine Lösung
ist möglich, wenn wir uns vergegenwärtigen, dass es für
Hoffmann *verschiedene 'Wirklichkeiten'* gibt, die überein-
ander geschichtet sind." (p. 40 f.) The "higher" realities
take on subjective forms, whereas the "lower" objective
reality of the everyday world loses importance and validity
as reality from the standpoint of the artist's world of the
marvelous and miraculous. I fully concur with this concept of the reality problem in Hoffmann's works, and it is
fundamental to the development of my discussions on his
myths. I cannot concur, however, with what appears to be
Dahmen's last word on Hoffmann's *Weltanschauung* in
his final chapter, entitled "Das Nordische bei Hoffmann,"
in which our author is described as the most Nordic of
German Romanticists. Furthermore, whether Hoffmann's
myths are of Southern or Northern origin is a question
that I regard as irrelevant to "new mythology."

The next comprehensive Hoffmann book was Ernst von

Schenck's *E. T. A. Hoffmann: Ein Kampf um das Bild des Menschen* (Berlin, 1939). This book is indeed a battle—as much for the reader as for the author. It must be conceded that von Schenck was correct in his attitude toward the subject as indicated by the subtitle: that great effort was needed to clear away the rubble left by former scholarship and popular prejudice. But the book does not fulfill the promise of the title. No clear image of Hoffmann, the man, emerges, for the author is at cross-purposes throughout. He claims his approach to be "sociological"—while attempting to analyze an individual man. Moreover, his ideas are often hopelessly entangled in a web of verbiage which conceals as much as it reveals. Von Schenck did, however, transcend biography, sociology, and his own pompous wordiness when discussing literary works, and demonstrates some originality in these discussions.

He regards Hoffmann's major works—and with this we must concur—as fundamentally mythical, and believes that Hoffmann attempted to create a new mythology. Von Schenck uses Plato's definition of myth: "eine Erzählung im Stile der Bildwelt, in der sich einem übersinnlichen Schauen eine rational nicht oder noch nicht fassbare Wirklichkeit offenbart." (p. XI) While I agree with all that "Bildwelt" here connotes, and that there is much irrationality involved in it, I would contend that there is still more sound rationale to it than is suggested here, and than von Schenck attributes to individual works. The very term *"world* of imagery" ("Bildwelt") points to interrelationships in imagery, which *are* "rational fassbar." As will be shown, these interconnections form a structure of their own on the basis of thematic association.[17] Within

---

[17] See also my dissertation (unpubl.), *Thematic Structure in Three Major Works of E. T. A. Hoffmann* (Princeton, 1957) for a detailed discussion of this principle of structure.

the mythical world, the functions of the central, recurring images are generally clear. What is not totally graspable is their *potential*. They possess a dynamic creative energy which points to infinite further possibilities. Such images as the golden pot, the bottle of the devil's elixir, or the "Urdarquelle" are *symbolic* in the sense described by August Wilhelm Schlegel: "Wie kann nun das Unendliche auf die Oberfläche, zur Erscheinung gebracht werden? Nur symbolisch, in Bildern und Zeichen. Die unpoetische Ansicht der Dinge ist die, welche mit den Wahrnehmungen der Sinne und den Bestimmungen des Verstandes alles an ihnen für abgethan hält; die poetische, welche sie immerfort deutet und eine figürliche Unerschöpflichkeit in ihnen sieht."[18] The indeterminate, unpredictable potential of Hoffmann's world of imagery is its main irrational aspect.

In applying the term "mythology," von Schenck proposes

eine Dreiheit der Gesichtsweisen zum Verständnis der Hoffmannschen Mythen: der kosmologische [Mythos], der das Ineinandersein von Mensch und Natur im weitesten Verstande schaut; der Mythos des radikalen und blossen Daseins als der des Verlorenseins in die vordergründige Profaneität der geschichtlich-sozialen Welt, den Hoffmann als den "Mythos des Bürgers" . . . wohl erstmals und original geschaut hat; schliesslich der Mythos des in der Zeit wiederhergestellten Menschseins, in dem zugleich die Überwindung und die Erfüllung des Mythischen überhaupt sich darstellt; hier findet die grundsätzliche Antithese zwischen Insein und Dasein ihre synthetische Aufhebung; folglich überwindet sich im "anthropologischen Mythos" die Mythik in sich selbst. (p. XII f.)

18 A. W. Schlegel, *Vorlesungen über schöne Litteratur und Kunst*, ed. J. Minor (Heilbronn, 1884), Erster Teil, p. 91.

This concept of myth has little in common with that of the Romantic tradition from which Hoffmann's myths evolved. Only the first "Gesichtsweise" seems applicable, although it is by no means exhaustive; "das Ineinandersein von Mensch und Natur" is certainly a state of mind of the artist who possesses and is possessed by Hoffmann's Romantic myth. But the "cosmological" myth does not contemplate ("schaut"); it *brings about* the process. Furthermore, von Schenck provides no attributes for the myth itself. The second point of view stands in flat contradiction to any concept of Romantic mythology. There can be no "Mythos des Bürgers" in Hoffmann, simply because "die vordergründige Profaneität der geschichtlich-sozialen Welt" is the very antithesis of Romantic myth. It is non-mythical, anti-mythical, sub-mythical—anything but mythical in terms of the "new mythology." The third point departs even further from what is actually the case. "Der Mythos des in der Zeit wiederhergestellten Mensch-seins" never really comes about except in a very limited sense. As will be seen in the chapter on *Kater Murr,* there appear late in Hoffmann's career many fragments of myth in the actual world—little tags which I choose to call "myth emblems": the separate unity of the mythical world, however, is left intact, and there is no "synthetische Aufhebung" of the antitheses involved.

In the same year as von Schenck's book there appeared a more specialized Hoffmann study that is of particular importance here: Kurt Willimczik's *E. T. A. Hoffmann: Die drei Reiche seiner Gestaltenwelt.* The book is based on the hypothesis that the mythical section of *Ritter Gluck* sums up the three basic "realms" for all the figures in Hoffmann's works: (1) "die breite Heerstrasse" (2) "Das Reich der Träume" (3) "Das Reich der Wahrheit."

As over-simplified as it may seem, this categorization has a certain limited validity. This is so because the myth of *Ritter Gluck* contains much that is fundamental to all of Hoffmann's mythical creations, hence to his whole literary art. Yet *Ritter Gluck* scarcely begins to exhaust the possibilities of its own Romantic myth. One would suspect this from the fact that *Ritter Gluck* was Hoffmann's very first literary work of any importance, written six years before his major poetic breakthrough when he conceived *Der goldne Topf*. The present study will, I believe, show that if any work is to be singled out and applied to all, then it should be *Der goldne Topf*. Still, Willimczik's study is revealing. Unfortunately the execution of his ideas falls below the brilliance of the conception. He is often sidetracked by belaborings of the master-apprentice relationship—a peripheral problem—and by certain notions associated with the ideology suggested by the title of the book.

The two comprehensive books on Hoffmann that have appeared in recent decades do not treat the question of mythology directly. They are those by Jean-F.-A. Ricci (Paris, 1947) and Harvey W. Hewett-Thayer (Princeton, 1948). Ricci's book is thorough and ends with some incisive conclusions on various topics (pp. 507-543). Myth is not an essential element in his treatment, however. He sees the myth of *Der goldne Topf* as "un conte mythique, sorte de résumé symbolique de l'histoire du monde. . . ." We have seen that Schelling had made a sharp distinction between the historical and the philosophical myth; and it will be shown that the historical aspects of Hoffmann's myths are scarcely significant. Hoffmann's myths are "philosophical," and transcend time.

Hewett-Thayer's book sums up the most significant

Hoffmann scholarship up to 1948. Like Harich, he frequently lapsed into straight renarration of the stories, but this is justified by his English-speaking audience for which translations of the majority of Hoffmann's works were not available. There is greater attention to analysis and interpretation in this work than in Harich's. The book provides in its short biography and several essays insights into many topics peripheral to this study: e.g., the occult, religion, and the *Märchen*.

An attempt at a brief, but comprehensive treatment of Hoffmann was made in recent years by Hans Mayer in his introduction to the edition of Hoffmann's *Poetische Werke* (Berlin, 1958), under the title *Die Wirklichkeit E. T. A. Hoffmanns. Ein Versuch.* This title might seem to suggest little discussion about such things as "myth." This is not the case, for Mayer regards the myth as "real": "Die Zweiteilung der Wirklichkeit als Dualität gegensätzlicher Raum- und Zeitvorstellungen durchzieht gerade die wichtigsten Werke des Erzählers Hoffmann . . . Es gibt zwei Wirklichkeiten in der Dichtung E. T. A. Hoffmanns." (p. X f.) One can scarcely deny this. It is necessary, however, to explain in what sense the mythical world is "real." The most broad-minded reader must be puzzled at first when he is expected to regard amorous, blue-eyed green snakes and salamander "Geisterfürsten" as real in any commonly accepted sense of the word. Mayer, from the beginning, simply puts them both into this category. While he does call Hoffmann's "Märchenwelt" a myth— even a "raum- und zeitlose Mythenwelt," we still have no justification for regarding them as "real" without further explanation. He might well have referred to Marianne Thalmann's important conclusion about what she calls Hoffmann's "Wirklichkeitsmärchen": "Stofflich dem

Mythos entnommen, werden diese eingelegten Märchen aber faktisch Ausdruck des Weltbewusstseins, das hinter unser enges Vordergrundsbewusstsein eingeschoben ist."[19] Although the question of realism is not the subject of this monograph, it lends some support to this "realistic" aspect of Hoffmann's literary art.

It is hoped that through a close study of his myths, Hoffmann's art will be shown to have the coherency and conclusiveness that Mayer denies it when he asserts, "Im allgemeinen . . . bleiben Hoffmanns Erzählungen ohne abschliessende Deutung und Rundung." (p. XV) Finally, it is contended that wider significance for Hoffmann's tales can be found than that indicated by Mayer's conclusion: "Das Gegeneinander der beiden Welten, der realen und der mythischen, erscheint als Ausdruck ungelöster deutscher Gesellschaftsverhältnisse. . . . Das Neben- und Ineinander der beiden Welten erweist sich . . . als Versuch einer Wirklichkeitsdeutung, die im Bereich ihrer Zeit und Zeitgenossen offenbar keine Möglichkeit sieht, die tiefen Lebenskonflikte anders als durch Ausweichen in den mythischen Bereich zu lösen." (p. XIX) Although there is doubtless a grain of truth in this, it is a grossly narrow view, and hardly reflects Hoffmann's intentions, whether stated, implicit, or subconscious. There is little evidence supporting the notion that, specifically, either changes in the social system or opposition to the course being taken by German history were fundamental to Hoffmann's thought. There is a far broader base of concern here—not "unresolved German social conditions," but *unredeemed civilized man*, a concept perhaps encompassing, but also transcending the compara-

[19] Marianne Thalmann, "E. T. A. Hoffmanns Wirklichkeitsmärchen," *Journal of English and Germanic Philology*, LI (1952), 488.

tively narrow social and national considerations by which
Mayer judges Hoffmann, thereby diminishing the cosmic
scope of his myths.

IV

Of the numerous specialized studies touching upon
mythology in Hoffmann, the most relevant are those of
Strich, Pfeiffer-Belli, and Martini.

In his section on Hoffmann in *Die Mythologie in der
deutschen Literatur* (II, 302 ff.), Strich discusses only *Der
goldne Topf* and *Das fremde Kind*. For its time (the
book was published in 1910) this is indeed a good beginning. His concept of the myth in *Der goldne Topf* centers
mainly on the "elemental spirits"—certainly a very basic
question. *Das fremde Kind*, treated very briefly, is a good
choice for extending his concept, yet several others could
just as well have been chosen. Strich does not, however,
treat Hoffmann's *Märchen* as embodiments of a "new
mythology," nor does he go into major aspects other than
the "Elementargeister." Yet, for the time when he wrote
this, when genuine literary scholarship on Hoffmann had
scarcely begun, his contribution is substantial.

An article, "Mythos und Religion bei E. T. A. Hoffmann," by W. Pfeiffer-Belli (1933) treats religion and
myth in Hoffmann's works as closely interrelated topics.
Pfeiffer-Belli pinpoints the places where Hoffmann's myths
are concentrated—in the primeval background stories of
his major *Märchen*. This is an important step which not
all critics take. He does not, however, relate it to the
theory of the new mythology, nor in any other way distinguish it as a peculiarly modern form of myth. Instead,
he interprets it as an expression of Christian doctrine on

the grounds that "allenthalben herrscht der Antagonismus lichter und finsterer Mächte" (p. 320). Granting this to be so, would this not rather make Hoffmann a devotee of Zoroastrianism?! Pfeiffer-Belli then proceeds along these lines by comparing the community of poets (a concept which is hardly developed in Hoffmann's myths) to the "unsichtbare Kirche."[20] The upshot of this interpretation is: "es ist phantastischer Theismus der dieser Märchenwelt zugrunde liegt," and that the end result of penetration into the world of myth is "bewusste Gotteskindschaft."

There is no evidence whatsoever for this interpretation of Hoffmann's *Märchen* myths. Theism and "Gotteskindschaft" are simply not the subject of these tales. In fact, a conscious antipathy toward conventional Christianity is manifested in *Der goldne Topf*. Anselmus is offended at being taken for a student of theology (I, 183: 21). And "Serpentina," the name of the figure of ideal beauty in the story, is "ein schnöder unchristlicher Name" in the eyes of the Philistine-type which Anselmus constantly encounters (I, 199: 1). One could possibly read a sense of piety toward nature into Hoffmann's myths, but little else along religious lines. Hoffmann's closest approximation to religious devotion in his myths is his endless glorification of the transcendent arts of music and poetry. One can, of course, look at this whole matter from a theological point of view and say that the apotheosis of art was Hoffmann's way of worshiping a deity. But this is not Hoffmann's point of view. It is true, as Hewett-Thayer perceived (pp. 121 ff.), that Hoffmann's Christian faith

---

[20] Hoffmann did speak of an "invisible church"—an esoteric community of artists—in critical works (e.g., XV, 35: 5 and V, 120: 6), but this idea is not incorporated into the myths: it is always an individual artist who enters the "other world," which is not populated by other poets, but by figures that are the subject of poetry.

was of overwhelming importance to him at certain critical points in his life. Furthermore, Roman Catholicism plays a great role in non-mythical sections of his works (*Die Elixiere des Teufels* and *Kater Murr*). But there is scarcely a trace of any devotion to a particular religious doctrine in his myths.

In his article, "Die Märchendichtungen E. T. A. Hoffmanns," Fritz Martini discusses the relationship of myth to *Märchen*, and comes to conclusions that are quite negative as far as the whole genre of *Kunstmärchen* is concerned (p. 63 f.). True myth, he claims, is possible only in a *Volksmärchen*, which operates according to a "Gesetzlichkeit des fraglos Mythischen . . . [die] ihre eigene Logik in sich besitzt." In contrast to this, the *Kunstmärchen* is described as a necessarily amorphous genre. Hoffmann's *Märchen* reflect in their language "Widersprüche . . . in denen er sich thematisch und weltanschaulich zwischen Sinnlichkeit und Transzendenz, fabulierendem Spiel und allegorischer Spekulation, Traum und Gedanke, Dichtung und Erkenntnis bewegt . . . es handelt sich bei ihm nicht um einen echten Mythos, sondern primär um in allegorische Anschauung gefasste weltanschauliche Spekulationen und um ein primär aesthetisches, ja geradezu ein artistisches Phaenomen" . . . "Man spricht . . . besser als vom Mythos von einer poetisch-spekulativen Mythologie, in der Mischung von Anschauung, Phantasie und Gedanken." While Martini's argument is persuasive in his own frame of reference, it does not apply completely to our present approach to mythology in Hoffmann. Martini may be quite right in denying that there is a "genuine myth" in Hoffmann by some definitions, for myth is a word used in many different ways. With the Romantic concept of *new mythology*, however, it is a different matter. Here—it is my contention—can be found the principles of myth-creation that make Hoffmann's *Märchen* more than the incoherent, fanciful game that they may appear to be superficially. Here can be found the "Gesetzlichkeit" that Martini apparently sought in vain in Hoffmann's *Märchen*.

v

The question of the new mythology in Hoffmann's works is a fundamental one. This is suggested by its importance for the Romantic tradition out of which Hoffmann grew, and the frequency with which Hoffmann critics have had to confront the problem in some way. It is, however, a problem that cannot be adequately treated in a few pages, as has been attempted before. Therefore this specialized study was undertaken.

In organizing the monograph, it was found most convenient and appropriate to combine two principles of ordering Hoffmann's numerous works: a chronological order combined with Hans von Müller's three categories of the "artistic," the "demonic," and the "fantastic" ("das Märchenhafte"). It is important that the intent of this book is understood to be a specialized study of a single problem, and that much relevant, but dispensible information was omitted for the sake of conciseness. It is hoped that in this manner the most clear and coherent image of Hoffmann's "new mythology" might emerge.

2

From Musician to Writer

Hoffmann's literary art emerged from music. This took place from about 1808 to 1813 when he was in his thirties and had matured as a musician. It is true that he had done considerable writing before this time, and that it amounted to more than a mere sideline. Even before the age of twenty, amidst various activities as an amateur musician and an occasional painter and sketcher, he found time to write a three-volume novel (*Cornaro*), part of another (*Der Geheimnisvolle*), to compose some verse, and to make plans for other literary works. Yet, from the little we know of these early works, most of which are not extant, it is doubtful whether much of Hoffmann's unique literary art was present in them. The two novels were apparently written under the influence of such works as Schiller's *Der Geisterseher*, emphasizing the occult and the fearsome. In the letters of his youth, typical features of his later writings are found only in embryonic form— as in musical metaphors and similes (e.g., *Briefwechsel*

I, 69 f. and 98). There is, however, no evidence of great originality until 1808, when it appeared suddenly in major proportions, only to remain in abeyance for five subsequent years.

In 1808 Hoffmann wrote *Ritter Gluck,* a novella which marked the initial and dramatic emergence of his career as a writer. It is with this work that some basic elements of Hoffmann's unique mythical world come forth in full clarity for the first time—a world from which the poetry of all his subsequent works can be derived.

It is helpful to know that *Ritter Gluck* was especially written for *Die allgemeine musikalische Zeitung,* for it bears a message for its specialized audience. The story conveyed: a revelation of the bad taste among Berlin musical circles and audiences; an encomium to C. W. von Gluck's genius as a composer; and certain ideas relating to the cosmic and absolute nature of music. The work, however, went even beyond these aims, for with it Hoffmann began to create the foundations for his Romantic myth.

The myth is contained in Gluck's vision of the transcendent realm of music (I, 27 f.). The way into it—i.e., the way to become a composer—leads through three areas: "die breite Heerstrasse," "das Reich der Träume," and "die Wahrheit." The first is the everyday world basking in its complacency and mediocrity. This is an especially appropriate image in the context of the story, for at the beginning the narrator has been sitting and watching the crowds of "die breite Heerstrasse" pass by. One enters into the next stage through the "ivory gate." Few are chosen to enter here. Behind the ivory gate there is color and adventure, but chaos. This realm is, however, closer to the center of the musical cosmos than the broad way. This is clearly a variation on Plato's allegory of the cave, with a lower degree of ignorance—that of "die breite Heerstrasse" —added to those observing the shadows on the wall. This realm of dreams behind the ivory gate, however, is only a midway station, although many can remain there forever as if in an eternal purgatory. The final step is into the eternal and ineffable truth centered on the sun, which Gluck interprets allegorically as "der Dreiklang, aus dem die Akkorde, Sternen gleich, herabschiessen und Euch mit Feuerfaden umspinnen."

It is a moment of glory for Gluck when he is drawn out of the fearsome darkness and chaos of the realm of dreams into the full brilliance of the sun's harmony. This occurs when he peers into a flower that grows and envelops him as it becomes the sun itself. (As will be seen later, flowers continued to bear a close symbolic relationship with the origins of life in Hoffmann's myths.) The sudden interruption in the narrative, which leaves ultimate truths undisclosed, comes about allegedly because the "Euphon"— the purest possible musical sound—rings in his ears. He is apparently being warned in an indirect way not to reveal the esoteric truths of his art. Furthermore, he is running away from a disturbing conversation that is partly about the poor musical creations and tastes prevalent in Berlin at that time. This conventional music is "lappländische Arbeit"—contrasted with the heat of the harmonious sun. Thus Gluck, in his flight, is not only attracted by the "sun" through the "Euphon," but is driven in that direction by the degradation of true music, including his own that is so badly played in this scene.

Yet Gluck can imagine true music when under the stimulus of even a poor imitation. This occurs in the above scene, and also later in the episode outside the opera when the narrator observes him listening in the darkness (as if in the realm of dreams), and giving a running account of the magnificent spectacle and sounds as he imagines them in their ideal form.

The ultimate, however, is reached in the final scene where Gluck plays his "true music" from blank note paper. Here he is completely removed from the "broad way" and all that it signifies. Here he can come as close to the "sun" as is feasible, and still be observed in actuality. The bizarreness of this scene manifests the absurd and paradoxical position of a genuine musician with respect to society: he is expected to express the inexpressible. In so doing he takes on the appearance of a madman, a ghost—even a desecrater of things most sacred to him. Thus it is dramatically shown that the transcendent realm of music is absolutely incommensurable with the "broad way."

There is more involved here than music, however. As is demonstrated by many of Hoffmann's later works, the "realm of the sun" is the central image of any art, even of the goal of all infinite strivings for absolutes of truth and beauty. This is the first known instance of a vision of a transcendent reality in Hoffmann's works. It is achieved through music, but the instrument for conveying it to us is here a literary form, requiring a translation of music into poetry. The tones and harmonies of a symphony are transformed into the images and structures of a verbal narrative. Images of light and darkness, phantoms, an abyss, the sun, giants, a sunflower correspond to musical sounds. The feelings and sensations out of which music originates—usually impossible to grasp and define in any other way—are here crystallized into images that can be perceived with other senses, mainly that of seeing.

The years in Hoffmann's artistic career known as the "Bamberg period" (1808-1813) are appropriately initiated by *Ritter Gluck*, for it was mainly during these years that he was developing his literary art by writing about music. There is a contradiction present in this process, for music remained supreme among the arts in his mind, but its supremacy was demonstrated most fully in certain sections of his musical writings that approach poetic rhapsodies— a form which competed in its artistry with its subject matter.

The poetic vocabulary which Hoffmann developed in this way is best illustrated by his review of Beethoven's *Fifth Symphony*, later revised and expanded into the essay, *Beethovens Instrumentalmusik*. Here Hoffmann again entered Gluck's realm of music through the medium of poetic words: "Die Musik schliesst dem Menschen ein unbekanntes Reich auf; eine Welt, die nichts gemein hat mit der äussern Sinnenwelt, die ihn umgibt, und in der er alle durch Begriffe bestimmbaren Gefühle zurücklässt, um sich dem Unaussprechlichen hinzugeben." Music does not reflect specific feelings and objects of experience. "Jede Leidenschaft . . . kleidet die Musik in den Purpurschimmer der Romantik, und selbst das im Leben Empfundene führt uns hinaus aus dem Leben und in das Reich des Unendlichen."

It should be noted here, however, that Hoffmann bestowed highly finite forms on this infinite art, although they are not those of common experience. This is illustrated in his discussions of specific works and composers, where he uses poetic images to describe them. To Haydn he attributes a realm consisting of "unabsehbare grüne Haine," containing features of a typical Rococo landscape. Mozart's infinite world is that of a "Geisterreich," at times fearsome, but ultimately pervaded with love and a beautiful melancholy.

Beethoven's realm is that of the monstrous and immeasureable: "Glühende Strahlen schiessen durch dieses Reiches tiefe Nacht, und wir werden Riesenschatten gewahr, die auf- und abwogen, enger und enger uns einschliessen und alles in uns vernichten, nur nicht den Schmerz der unendlichen Sehnsucht, in welcher jede Lust, die schnell in jauchzenden Tönen emporgestiegen, hinsinkt und untergeht, und nur in diesem Schmerz, der, Liebe, Hoffnung, Freude in sich verzehrend, aber nicht zerstörend, unsre Brust mit einem vollstimmigen Zusammenklange aller Leidenschaften zersprengen will, leben wir fort und sind entzückte Geisterseher." The similarity of this passage to the vision in *Ritter Gluck* is immediately apparent. In this case, however, it is not an utterance by a man whose sanity and reality is suspect, but by a music critic introducing a rather scientific and technical analysis. Such a context suggests increased self-confidence. He himself is approaching the advanced stage of artistic development attributed to Beethoven with this most impressive image in the passage: "Er trennt sein Ich von dem inneren Reich der Töne und gebietet darüber als unumschränkter Herr." To apply this to the later Hoffmann as writer, one need only substitute "words and images" for "Töne."

Somewhat more artistic in a generic sense are the Kreisler fragments—little fictional sketches about his literary self-image, the tortured *Kapellmeister* Johannes Kreisler who eventually succumbs to insanity. These fragments do not, however, contain much that is directly related to the myth that he had begun to create in *Ritter Gluck*, but they constitute a revealing personal background of the type of Romantic artist who would be inclined toward the mythical. There is an occasional flash of this kind of poetry, but for the most part, it is the very lack of such beauty that is the point in the bleak milieu in which Kreisler must practice his art of music. He is the epitome of the frustrated musician who possesses everything he needs to make music—except the opportunity to do so. His social environment is hostile to genuine music, and he is therefore constantly yearning for the glorious other world of music—which, however, is never described as in *Ritter Gluck* and *Beethovens Instrumentalmusik*. The Kreisler fragments as a whole present a complex set of problems that are not altogether relevant here; therefore only a few points about them must suffice.

Kreisler is a musician, and only a musician. It is a calling that makes absolute demands, Hoffmann's concept of music being what it is. Kreisler's devotion to his art is correspondingly absolute. His role as such a musician is in complete conflict with his role in society as a music teacher, performer, and composer. These roles make his position absurd in his own eyes, for his audience either does not listen to the best that he has to offer (*Johannes Kreislers musikalische Leiden*) or listens for the most ludicrous reasons—for "educational" considerations, moral edification, social status, etc. (*Ueber den hohen Wert der Musik.*)

What is fundamentally lacking in Kreisler's life is a concreteness, a sensual immediacy which the "ethereal," impalpable, barely definable art of music does not bear for him. This vacuum could possibly be filled by a sympathetic social milieu, but he is usually met with coldness or hostility in his audience. The one great exception is his ideal beloved, a young music pupil in whom his musical aspirations are fulfilled. She remains, however, inaccessible to him except when they share their music.

The agonizing dichotomy of his ideal and actual roles is

scarcely bearable. Hoffmann himself was somewhat more fortunate than his literary self-image, for he had other roles to turn to: that of writer, painter, theater technician, and civil servant.[1] Only on a few occasions does Kreisler turn to the main one of these: writing poetic confessions. Kreisler remains in his misery, continuing on his way to insanity, but Hoffmann emerges from the depths of despair by putting Kreisler into a poetic context—without making him primarily a poet.

There are a few interesting exceptions where Kreisler approaches a poetic myth derived from music. In the third fragment of *Höchst zerstreute Gedanken*, Kreisler, as author of the work, speaks of the "Übereinkunft der Farben, Töne und Düfte" which he imagines after having heard music. "Es kömmt mir vor, als wenn alle auf die gleiche geheimnisvolle Weise durch den Lichtstrahl erzeugt würden und dann sich zu einem wundervollen Konzerte vereinigen müssten.—Der Duft der dunkelroten Nelken wirkt mit sonderbar magischer Gewalt auf mich; unwillkürlich versinke ich in einen träumerischen Zustand und höre dann wie aus weiter Ferne die anschwellenden und wieder verfliessenden tiefen Töne des Bassetthorns." The relationship of the creative "Lichtstrahl" to the sun myth in *Ritter Gluck* is apparent. Thus the embryo of Hoffmann's myth is present in Kreisler's slight poetic talent.

Kreisler's interest in the poetic is further demonstrated by frequent reference to "poets and musicians" or "poets and artists." These juxtapositions indicate common denominators. In the twelfth of the *Höchst zerstreute Gedanken* Kreisler uncovers something that is one of the

---

[1] This applies only to the early Kreisler fragments. In the later Kreisler story in *Kater Murr*, we learn that he had been a civil servant, but turned away from the position in despair.

roots of all the arts. Here he speaks of the "inspiration" that some musicians *and* poets gain from "spirits"—the alcoholic kind. Kreisler finds a particular variety exceptionally effective—one that is sugared, then ignited. "Die Bereitung und der mässige Genuss dieses Getränkes hat für mich etwas Wohltätiges und Erfreuliches.—Wenn so die blaue Flamme emporzuckt, sehe ich, wie die Salamander glühend und sprühend herausfahren und mit den Erdgeistern kämpfen, die im Zucker wohnen. Diese halten sich tapfer; sie knistern in gelben Lichtern durch die Feinde, aber die Macht ist zu gross, sie sinken prasselnd und zischend unter—die Wassergeister entfliehen, sich im Dampfe emporwirbelnd, indem die Erdgeister die erschöpften Salamander herabziehen, und im eignen Reiche verzehren. . . ." He then recommends a list of various beverages, each having a quality peculiarly appropriate to a particular kind of musical composition!

The source of the above is a genuine traditional myth—the elemental spirits which haunted many of the German Romanticists.[2] Although these figures are used facetiously here, they are often of serious import in later works, when they take on far greater dimensions. They embody certain forces and basic materials in nature, from which the poet may draw in creating his own artistic world.

There is a gap in Hoffmann's fully-formed poetic works from *Ritter Gluck* (1808) to near the end of the Bamberg period, shortly before the writing of *Der goldne Topf* (1813). During this time he wrote almost nothing but musical criticism. Then two genuinely poetic works appeared: *Don Juan* and *Die neuesten Schicksale des Hundes Berganza.*

Don Juan is a further development of the Kreisler

---

[2] Cf. Oswald Floeck's *Die Elementargeister bei Fouqué und anderen Dichtern der romantischen und nachromantischen Zeit* (Heidelberg, 1909).

motifs. Its subject is music and its supra-real nature, but it does not contain a myth. *Berganza* is a loosely-constructed prose piece in its genre and artistic aim, but contains some new features that bore much fruit in later works. This dialogue, a nocturnal conversation between a dog and a man, is Hoffmann's first extended use of both the dialogue form and the animal figure as a mirror for human beings. Hoffmann's mythical world is populated with almost as many animals as human beings. In colorful variations, they appear as grotesque and whimsical figurations of fundamental human and natural forms. The creation of Berganza is the first step toward the hilarious autobiography of a tomcat in *Kater Murr*. Finally, there is an extended passage—the story of Berganza's escape from Cannizares—which develops motifs of Hoffmann's grotesque and sinister demonry: witches, the occult, black magic in a midnight setting, etc. Thus *Berganza*, although not a major work in itself, constituted a major advancement toward Hoffmann's finding himself as a writer.

In summing up the reasons for Hoffmann's transformation from musician to writer—a complex subject indeed—one should first consider the suffering that his role as a musician caused him, and lack of motivation for continuing in it. There was also his unfortunate love for his vocal pupil, Julia Marc. In addition to the obvious problems associated with a married man's love for a girl just entering womanhood, Hoffmann had to witness her being practically sold into a marriage of convenience with a man whose vileness seems beyond question. The necessity for a separation from her meant the loss of the person to whom his music was dedicated, and with whom he shared it in performances. This act of renunciation apparently caused the crystallization of an inward image that needed a more visible representation than music could possibly offer. Accompanying these painful events was a project which, in a more positive way, was symptomatic of the transition from one art to the other. This was the composition of the music to the opera *Undine* in collaboration with Fouqué. Although Hoffmann had composed music for operas before, this was a special event, for here was doubtless the libretto that was most congenial to him. It was based on mythical figures—the elemental spirits—which were a major addition to Hoffmann's mythical world. In *Undine*, a primeval world of elemental spirits is revealed and activated. The charming feminine figure, Undine, a water-sprite that takes on human form, bears much resemblance to Serpentina in *Der goldne Topf*.

The transition from music to poetry was further encouraged when Hoffmann left Bamberg for his short but critical period in Leipzig and Dresden. In fact, the experiences here were such that it is scarcely an exaggeration to say that Hoffmann was driven to poetry. The Julia crisis was only the beginning of this process. His role as a musician, instead of being improved by this move, was worsened to the point where he was forced to resign under the exploitation and insults of Seconda, the director of the opera company in which Hoffmann was the orchestra director. Associated with these troubles was the general insecurity of his position, for he had to move back and forth between Leipzig and Dresden within a few months. Added to these woes were the poverty, hunger, lonelinesss, and illness that he and his wife had to bear. Hoffmann had unwittingly leaped right into the area in which the most chaotic and fearsome war activities of his time were taking place.

"In keiner, als in dieser düstern verhängnisvollen Zeit,

wo man seine Existenz von Tage zu Tage fristet und ihrer froh wird, hat mich das Schreiben so angesprochen." (Hoffmann's letter to Kunz, Dresden, Aug. 19, 1813.) This impressive announcement heralds Hoffmann's total conversion to poetry as his primary art. The letter accompanies the story, *Der Magnetiseur*, and announces plans for the tale which a few months later evolved into *Der goldne Topf*. In sharp contrast to these activities in an ideal realm of art, this same letter contains descriptions of the frightful war conditions. Thus Hoffmann's literary art is here a compensatory kind, which provides a cosmic order and beauty lacking in daily life, and for which he and his German contemporaries were yearning. Hoffmann did utilize some of his war experiences for some minor literary works (*Der Dichter und der Komponist, Drey verhängnissvolle Monathe!, Die Vision auf dem Schlachtfelde*). In these works, there is occasionally some of the ambiguous feeling summed up in his diary entry of Oct. 11, 1813, where he describes the burning of French barracks as "ein grässlich schönes Schauspiel." Far more predominant, however, is the *un*ambiguous attitude on August 29, 1813: "Was ich so oft im Traume gesehen ist mir erfüllt worden—auf furchtbare Weise—Verstümmelte zerrissene Menschen!!"

To remove his thoughts from these horrors he cultivated his innate interest in such things as the occult, the fantastic, and most successfully, the mythical. In *Der Magnetiseur* he delved into "animal magnetism," a popular subject of the day. This story is not among Hoffmann's best, for it remains in the realm of mystification without probing deeply into the cosmic areas that the occult can symbolize. Nevertheless, this story is also important in his development toward the writing of *Der goldne Topf* and other works, mainly because there are certain character types that had hitherto not been successfully portrayed. There is Alban, the mysterious hypnotist wielding his evil power over Auguste, the epitome of maidenly charm; and there is Franz Bickert, the master artist whose wisdom and intelligence place him in the superior position of the man who has learned to control his milieu as he controls his art. Such forceful master figures had not yet appeared in Hoffmann's writings. Another story, *Die Automate,* written before the completion of *Der goldne Topf,* treats a similar theme: power wielded by a sinister master figure (Professor X) by means of a prophetic talking mannikin, "der redende Türke." These two stories do not present Hoffmann's myth as such, but begin to develop that area of it associated with the master figure. Also Hoffmann is already able to visualize the new development of his myth accurately in terms of the *Urzeit* (using, however, the words of G. H. von Schubert): "In jener Urzeit des menschlichen Geschlechts, als es . . . in der ersten heiligen Harmonie mit der Natur lebte, erfüllt von dem göttlichen Instinkt der Weissagung und Dichtkunst, als der Geist des Menschen nicht die Natur, sondern diese den Geist des Menschen erfasste, und die Mutter das wunderbare Wesen, das sie geboren, noch aus der Tiefe ihres Daseins nährte, da umfing sie den Menschen wie im Wehen einer ewigen Begeisterung mit heiliger Musik, und wundervolle Laute verkündeten die Geheimnisse ihres ewigen Treibens." (VI, 94 f.) This passage from *Die Automate* shows Hoffmann in the border area of the myth of *Der goldne Topf.*

He was now about to embark on the main part of his literary career lasting nine years and cut short by his death. During this time he wrote stories which here are best divided into three groupings, presenting his Romantic myth from three different perspectives: (1) tales of the Romantic artist, the instrument of myth (2) tales of the Satanic and the underworld, originating from the chaotic and destructive forces of the mythical world, and opposing the higher creative principle (3) *Kunstmärchen*, tales employing a background myth which contains an all-embracing primeval cosmos asserting itself in modern times. These groups are not mutually exclusive. In fact, all three have their bases in Hoffmann's first major literary work, *Der goldne Topf*.

3

Der Goldne Topf:
The Cosmic Myth

"Es ist, als schlösse ich mir ein wunderbares Reich auf, das aus meinem Innern hervorgehend und sich gestaltend mich dem Drange des Äussern entrückte." (Hoffmann's letter to Kunz, August 19, 1813.) Under the spell of this experience Hoffmann wrote his most fully-developed mythical work, *Der goldne Topf*. This passage also is an accurate description of what happens in *Der goldne Topf* itself to the hero, Anselmus; for the work tells of the "Bildung" of the poet, the process whereby the "wunderbares Reich" of poetry is opened up to a young man whose previous life has been so empty that it is extremely susceptible to being suddenly filled with some kind of myth, like a vacuum about to be filled by violent implosion.

During the years 1812 and 1813 Hoffmann, like Anselmus, his Parzival-like "tumber," had undergone a rapid development which led his imagination into his own fantastic realm of myth. Hoffmann's own experience is reflected when Anselmus is subjected to a constant conflict between the world of everyday and the insubstantial, but gloriously beautiful poetic world to which the master-figure Archivarius Lindhorst introduces him. But this is only part of the biographical aspect of the story, for by the very act of creating the tale, Hoffmann wields power—like Lindhorst—over the mythical realm. We can feel Hoffmann's exhilaration over his own poetic powers when he noted in his diary: "gemüthlicher Geburtstags Abend—sich in eigner Glorie gesonnt und was auf sich selbst ge-h[alten]." (Jan. 24, 1814.) This is not an Anselmus speaking through Hoffmann, but a Lindhorst—a master, not an apprentice, of myth. Thus in *Der goldne Topf* Hoffmann presents certain aspects of his own character separate from one another, and allows them to interact independently. This interaction is the starting-point of a phenomenon which takes on cosmic dimensions, and involves a vision of huge dynamic energies that go far beyond Hoffmann's psychological make-up.

Hoffmann's creation of *Der goldne Topf* was a sudden breakthrough. This is reflected in the beginning of the story itself when the poetic world suddenly enters Ansel-mus' life and upsets the applecart in more than a figurative sense, when he runs into Liese's fruit-stand. Anselmus' equilibrium is destroyed from the shock of this initial breakthrough. Then the higher realm—along with a new love—enters in the "Holunderbaum" scene by the Elbe. After this, the conflict of the mythical world with his everyday life arises in connection with Veronika and the Philistine types with whom she is associated. Finally the battle being waged between the higher and lower forces in the myth—embodied in Liese and Lindhorst—is seen when Anselmus attempts to gain entry into Lindhorst's house, and is forcibly stopped by her. This incident is followed immediately by the full force of the breakthrough, Lindhorst's story of the *Urzeit*, at the beginning of the third *Vigilie*. The sudden plunge into a far-away myth reflects artistically the precipitousness of the breakthrough. There is also something melodramatic about this beginning, which in combination with the high-flown rhetorical style conveys a subtle irony about the narrator, who has the appearance of an odd duck and a charlatan in the eyes of the Philistine society to whom it is told. Essentially, however, the myth is to be taken seriously. Hoffmann himself appeals to the reader to do so in the next *Vigilie*—to behold the "countenance of the earnest goddess." The irony in her smile is no more than "der neckhafte Scherz, der in allerlei verwirrendem Zauber mit uns spielt, so wie die Mutter oft mit ihren liebsten Kindern tändelt" (I, 194: 17). The irony with which Hoffmann treats his myths —powerful as it is—should not be over-emphasized to the point where their serious side is destroyed.

The beginning of Lindhorst's tale is a highly concentrated expression of Hoffmann's mythical vision of the *Urzeit*. "Der Geist schaute auf das Wasser, da bewegte es sich und brauste in schäumenden Wogen und stürzte sich donnernd in die Abgründe, die ihren schwarzen Rachen aufsperrten, es gierig zu verschlingen." The substance and biblical style of this passage are, of course, strongly reminiscent of the Creation. This source is, however, greatly modified and artistically formed, as we shall see, and the differences which emerge are more important than the similarities. The first step in Hoffmann's version of the Creation is the activation of three basic substances by their contact with one another—spirit, water, and darkness. These constitute, respectively, a higher, a middle, and a

lower realm. All three are necessary parts of the interaction, although the initial impulse comes from the spirit,
as is made clear in the very first phrase. The action which
ensues is one of vast cosmic force, whereby the water of
the middle realm is caused by the spirit to react in a
violent manner with the depths, and seems to be threat-
ened by them. This brings about an act of creation which
is the prototype for similar phenomena later in the story:
"Wie triumphierende Sieger hoben die Granitfelsen ihre
zackicht gekrönten Häupter empor, das Tal schützend,
bis es die Sonne in ihren mütterlichen Schoss nahm und,
es umfassend, mit ihren Strahlen wie mit glühenden
Armen pflegte und wärmte." This step is a further development of the original triadic scheme. Out of the violent
interaction are produced the cliffs, which arise from the
depths, and protect the valley (a middle area) on which
the sun shines (corresponding to the spirit).

Thus far the triadic scheme is extremely simple. From
this point on, however, such exact and clear-cut equations
can no longer be made on any large scale, for all new
products of creation come about only as a result of a
unique kind of *interaction*, and they therefore bear features stemming from two or even three of these areas.
With each new step in the progressive process of creation
which ensues, this interweaving becomes more and more
intricate, and causes more and more ambivalences, as can
be seen in the continuation of this passage: "Da erwachten
tausend Keime, die unter dem öden Sande geschlummert,
aus dem tiefen Schlafe und streckten ihre grüne Blättlein
und Halme zum Angesicht der Mutter hinauf, und wie
lächelnde Kinder in grüner Wiege ruhten in den Blüten
und Knospen Blümlein, bis auch sie, von der Mutter
geweckt, erwachten und sich schmückten mit den Lich-

tern, die die Mutter ihnen zur Freude auf tausendfache
Weise bunt gefärbt."

The first plant-life arises, then, from the seeds sleeping
under sand, which, as it is described here with the
adjective "öd," would seem to be related to the lower
realm. As the plants grow, however, it is the higher order,
embodied in the sun, which furthers their growth. Then
a new development takes place. "Aber in der Mitte des
Tals war ein schwarzer Hügel, der hob sich auf und nieder
wie die Brust des Menschen, wenn glühende Sehnsucht
sie schwellt.—Aus den Abgründen rollten die Dünste
empor, und sich zusammenballend in gewaltige Massen,
strebten sie das Angesicht der Mutter feindlich zu verhül-
len; die rief aber den Sturm herbei, der fuhr zerstäubend
unter sie, und als der reine Strahl wieder den schwarzen
Hügel berührte, da brach im Übermass des Entzückens
eine herrliche Feuerlilie hervor, die schönen Blätter wie
holdselige Lippen öffnend, der Mutter süsse Küsse zu
empfangen." The combining of the lower and higher
realms here is seen in the interaction of darkness (the
black hill) with "Sehnsucht," which is a potential power
of creativity, resembling the initial impulse of the spirit.
This manifestation of spirit provides the impetus for another triadic interaction, when the vapors of the lower
world challenge the creative activity of the higher, and
the wind of the middle realm is called upon to disperse
the destructive element. The result of this process of
challenge and response is again a higher form of life—
the fire-lily—which is richer, more vital, and more beautiful than anything that has previously existed. The fire-lily,
from this point on, appears frequently and at significant
places in the story as a symbol associated with creativity—
for example as adornment on Lindhorst's dressing gown,

and as part of Anselmus' dowry, growing out of the golden pot. At the end of this passage we see a highly concentrated form of life expressing itself in love (for the mother), which soon thereafter is lavished on Phosphorus, the lily's lover.

This love, a basic creative urge, sets off a further conflict of fundamental forces in the middle world. The lily possesses something new for the creatures of her environment, "der Gedanke," a power which initiates vital action, bringing about tensions, conflicts, and their resolutions. Like the black hill, the lily is apparently intended to be a prototype of man, the difference between the two being that the fire-lily possesses a greater concentration of vital energy in her "Gedanke" than the hill in its "Sehnsucht." At this point, the race of mythical creatures later inhabiting the primeval world begins to appear, and forms part of the background of the love-affair of Phosphorus and the lily. Variations on previous motifs and images are presented in a rapid and complex development, thus departing from the focal origin of the myth.

The fundamental forces which are indicated here, and their interactions, could be traced throughout the remainder of the mythical section of the story contained in Lindhorst's narration, then in its continuation told by Serpentina in the eighth *Vigilie*, as well as in other sections of the story where mythical elements appear. The passage that has been cited should suffice, however, as a point of reference to which all these motifs can be traced. Life-processes become more and more intricate, and individual phenomena and forces combine with each other in ever-increasing variations, so that the question of distinguishing between higher, middle, and lower realms leads to more and more ambivalences. Yet the small, individual parts of the subsequent myth clearly indicate their origin by means of some concrete characteristic. It is their *combination* which causes bewilderment—a bewilderment that stems from profound insights into the world as experienced by Hoffmann at the time, and somewhat as experienced by Kleist twelve years before Hoffmann wrote *Der goldne Topf*: "Tausendfältig verknüpft und verschlungen sind die Dinge der Welt, jede Handlung ist die Mutter von Millionen andern, und oft die schlechteste erzeugt die besten. . . ." (Letter of August 15, 1801, to Wilhelmine von Zenge.) The artistic expression of such a world-view would tend to be centered on clusters of concrete, but ambivalently associated symbols.

The difficulty that this might cause for the reader of *Der goldne Topf* is greatly lessened if their origin in the central myth is kept clearly in mind. Furthermore, it is also helpful to be aware of Hoffmann's technique of developing the substances of this myth—a technique originating in music. One of the most highly developed aspects of Hoffmann's musical theory was his analysis of thematic structure.[1] This has a bearing on his literary art. It can be shown by extremely detailed investigation that large groups of the "themes"—i.e., objects, sensual qualities, motifs, etc.—in Hoffmann's literary works are related and formed by this very principle of thematic association.[2] *Der goldne Topf* is the prime example of such association, mainly because of its complex but distinct pattern of themes which have their origin and meaning in the central myth. To illustrate this pattern, two figures, with whom the most perplexing combinations of themes are associated,

---

[1] Cf. Paul Greeff, *E. T. A. Hoffmann als Musiker und Musikschriftsteller* (Köln und Krefeld, 1948), p. 114.
[2] See Introd., note 17.

should suffice as examples. They are Lindhorst and Liese, the protagonists in the battle of the primeval world being waged around Anselmus.

Archivarius Lindhorst is primarily an instrument of the higher purposes of the primeval middle world, for his role in the story is to engender poetic creativity in Anselmus— to bring about a higher and more productive form of life than Anselmus' previous one, just as the sun had brought forth and nurtured the fire-lily on the black hill that had been filled with "Sehnsucht." The motifs with which Lindhorst is usually associated are manifestations of the higher order. Outstanding among these are the light and fire of the sun: Lindhorst is, after all, "in reality" a salamander, traditionally the external form of the ele- mental spirit of fire. Throughout the story a great number of concrete objects and actions originate in this "element" —such as his ability to light a pipe by snapping his fingers, the bright sparkle of his magic ring, and the flaming lilies which he uses as weapons against Liese. He is also associated with luxuriant plant-life (of which the fire-lily is the prototype), for his exotic study-room is filled with tropical trees and flowers; his dressing gown is adorned with flowers; and "der goldne Topf" itself contains a fire- lily when it is presented to Anselmus as a dowry. All that these particular themes represent in connection with the central myth converges on the point where Lindhorst ap- pears to Anselmus in the form of a "Geisterfürst" (I, 211), a being that dominates and controls with creative power and intent.

On the other hand, Lindhorst cannot be a *perfect* mem- ber of a primeval world ruled by the higher realm, for if he were, there would be no justification for his being placed among "das entartete Geschlecht der Menschen," as we are called at one point in the story (I, 222). His proper station would be in Atlantis. Thus there are some features of Lindhorst which lower him somewhat in the hierarchy of the primeval world. Therefore he has also a demonic side which on a few occasions makes him appear threatening and even destructive. This characteristic can be traced largely to his forced exile from Atlantis to the world of men for having destroyed a flower garden in a moment of mad anguish after losing his beloved. Thus for the time being he is a fallen angel doing penance.

The possibility of such a misfortune lies in his essential make-up as a salamander. This creature is not only associated with the fire and light of the higher world, but also with some of the figures of the lower world in the category of black flying dragons, and other grotesque animals. (It would follow from this, then, that Serpentina has at least a touch of the demonic in her, expressed in her external appearance as a snake.) This aspect of Lindhorst, along with its appropriate imagery, appears most clearly when Anselmus sees him fly away in the form of a bird of prey, at a moment when the young student is confused and uncertain with regard to Lindhorst (I, 198). The "Geisterfürst" Lindhorst *must* at times appear to be a threat to Anselmus, for he cannot avoid destroying Anselmus' connections with the unproductive areas of the conventional world. On the whole, however, the destructive factors in Lindhorst are peripheral, or are associated only with the fact that most of his actions in the story take place in the modern world, to which the structure and values of his original world are foreign.

Liese is the exact counterpart of Lindhorst: she is primarily a creature of the underworld, but has certain peripheral attributes of the higher levels of the primeval cosmos. The principal themes with which she is associated are those connoting darkness, grotesqueness, and destruction. Therefore she works hand-in-hand with the Philistine world, which is the greatest threat to Anselmus' destiny as a poet. Most of the motifs characterizing her converge in the fifth *Vigilie*, when Veronika visits this phenomenally ugly creature. Here Liese is dressed in black rags, and lives in a dark, chaotic abode, teeming with grotesque animals, and filled with the paraphernalia of a witch's kitchen. The conjuration scene in the seventh *Vigilie*, shrouded in darkness, also shows her in a milieu typical of the underworld. Furthermore, her general role and significance have a mythical basis in the second part of the myth in the eighth *Vigilie* (I, 223: 39). Here we learn that she is the offspring of a romance between a black feather from the wing of an underworld dragon, and a beet root. The latter, subterranean type of vegetable—suggestive of a mandrake root—is associated with the lower realm, and forms a contrast to Lindhorst's flowers and tropical plants growing above ground. Liese's origin has far-reaching significance for Hoffmann's mythology as a whole, for her provenance from the lower depths—a necessary part of the primal world—provides a kind of mythical vindication for the existence of evil.

Yet Liese, at certain points, has some superficial resemblances to the higher part of Lindhorst's being. In fact, there is a rather long list of parallel images which include most of the major themes associated with these two figures. The witch's cauldron is the counterpart of "der goldne Topf"—with regard to its general category of a receptacle, its three-legged stand, its connection with marriage, and its central position in the incantation scene. Liese's magic mirror has much the same function as Lindhorst's magic ring—that of a kind of crystal ball. The unruly animals in her dwelling can be equated with the impertinent parrots in Lindhorst's. Also light and fire are associated with her, but of a lesser brightness than Lindhorst's, and casting an eerie rather than a radiant glow over the surroundings. The whole parallel is summed up when Liese says to Veronika: "Er ist der weise Mann, aber ich bin die weise Frau." (I, 205.) Since the two compete with one another in a middle sphere between their original realms, they must, it seems, have some common denominators in order to be true competitors. Also, the ambivalence in the two figures is a necessary outcome of their origin in the mythical middle realm, where higher and lower powers are inseparably fused.

The relationship of the central myth and the *everyday world* is not so intimate as that between opposing realms in the myth. The mythical origin of all things is either too far removed from our world to have any connection with it, or it comes into conflict with it. This clash is most abrupt where Lindhorst is unceremoniously interrupted in his telling of the myth by the words, "Erlauben Sie, das ist orientalischer Schwulst, werter Herr Archivarius!" It is significant that this is said by Registrator Heerbrand, for he is the caricature of the arch-Philistine in the story, embodying mainly "social" values carried to their ridiculous extreme.[3] In the eyes of this man, the cosmic forces acting and reacting in the myth are meaningless, for his main concerns are such problems as his relative social rank, its bearing on the marriage market, and short-cut methods of remembering the location of misplaced documents.

His basic estrangement from myth is paradoxically

[3] For a revealing categorization of Hoffmann's Philistine types, cp. P. Bruning's "E.T.A. Hoffmann and the Philistine," *German Quarterly*, XXVIII (1955), 111-121. Although the three groups (the smug Philistine, the demonic type, and the "Bildungsphilister") apply in most other cases, they could lead to an oversimplification of Heerbrand's uniquely complex role as a Philistine in *Der goldne Topf*.

underscored by his very proximity to it, for although he, like Anselmus, has ample opportunity to experience it, he fails consistently to recognize its value. The many parallels between him and Anselmus serve only to bring out their fundamental differences. Both have "einen Hang zu den *Poeticis* . . . und da verfällt man leicht in das Phantastische und Romanhafte." Both derive "inspiration" from alcohol (as also the author does at the end of the story). Both enjoy a close relationship with Lindhorst. In fact, it is Heerbrand who arranges the meetings between Anselmus and Lindhorst. Both are in love with Veronika, and, as the story evolves, hope to reach the goal of marriage with her via the social position of a "Hofrat."

As with Lindhorst and Liese, however, these two competitors for Veronika's hand are oriented from two opposite poles. Heerbrand's "Hang zu den *Poeticis*" is motivated ultimately by purely professional and visceral considerations. His interest in "spirits" is nothing but a borderline dipsomania that twice causes him to make an utter fool of himself (I, 224 f. and 228); whereas Anselmus' somewhat lesser indulgences are associated with a penetration into the mythical depths of his experience. As for Heerbrand's association with Lindhorst, he fails to see the forest for the trees: the "Archivarius" in his eyes is a man "with connections"; here appears his purely Philistine respect for rank. To be sure, he finds Lindhorst entertaining, but where Lindhorst's mythical salamander identity comes to the fore, as with the magic fire-trick, Heerbrand immediately takes recourse to the sober, rationalistic explanation in the words, "Sehen Sie das chemische Kunststückchen." Only when Heerbrand is thoroughly inebriated in the ninth *Vigilie* does he admit that Lindhorst is "really" a Salamander. But the hilarious madness of this scene makes it exceptional, and scarcely allows Heerbrand's statement to be taken seriously. Finally, Heerbrand's and Anselmus' common love for Veronika lends emphasis to their diverging paths at the end. Heerbrand wins the girl, but Anselmus gains her gloriously beautiful artistic reflection in the mythical figure of Serpentina.

Heerbrand, then, must be regarded as the arch-Philistine counterpart of Anselmus, a concentrated and exaggerated form of all the people of his immediate conventional environment: Veronika; her father; Konrektor Paulmann; the solid citizen and his wife who bring Anselmus back to "reality" in the "Holunderbaum" scene; even the whole society of Anselmus' immediate surroundings at the beginning of the story, when he makes an unsuccessful attempt to become a part of it. He is also Anselmus' distorted self-image, as it appears to Philistine society.

The modern world, as experienced at this point in Hoffmann's life, has little to do with the mythical cosmos. The mythical middle realm should not, therefore, be equated with the immediate world of actuality. The humdrum everyday of the Philistine is at best only a distortion of the myth, for it has been uprooted and displaced from its origin. Therefore it should be regarded as a *fourth* area to be added to the three evolving immediately from the central myth. This fourth realm cannot, as Hoffmann depicts it here, provide the vital, natural, primal materials which are those of Romantic poetry. Therefore a work that is "poetic" in Hoffmann's sense of the word must rest on mythical hypothesis, created out of the depths of the writer's mind, on which the total meaning of his individual character and of the essential nature of the world, as he has experienced it, come to a focal point. In this sense, the myth of the *Urzeit* gains actuality in the present. Here much of Friedrich Schlegel's proposal for a new mythology is fulfilled.

The central myth of the third and eighth *Vigilie* does not remain static and limited. Its potential is not exhausted by what is contained in a few pages of prose, because it is, as it were, charged with an energy that has infinite application. The world—the one that is fundamental for Hoffmann—is activated by this energy, and is allowed to combine and interweave the elements so that all is one grandiose panorama, constantly changing its appearance through variations of light and darkness, height and depth, angelic and demonic, good and evil, creativity and destructiveness. This is the "beautiful chaos" of Romantic mythology.

There is, of course, a great deal of immoderation in all this, because the underlying world-view is immoderate. There are perhaps some passages in *Der goldne Topf* where, for some readers, the unlimited energies that are released seem to bring about pointless increase in free association. This is a matter of taste. At the end, at least, these energies are brought under perfect control. After Anselmus has permanently entered the eternally poetic realm of Atlantis, Hoffmann states with assertiveness and finality: "Ist denn überhaupt des Anselmus Seligkeit etwas anderes als das Leben in der Poesie, der sich der heilige Einklang aller Wesen als tiefstes Geheimnis der Natur offenbaret?" After a richly embellished sequence of dissonances, the *Kapellmeister* Hoffmann, now also a master of the narrative art, demonstrated his ability to resolve a huge array of themes into one great harmony. He achieved this by creating, in Friedrich Schlegel's sense, a "Mittelpunkt" and "Urquell" of the poetic in his own myth.

4

The Romantic Artist

As the musician in Hoffmann became less and less active
due to the poetic breakthrough of *Der goldne Topf,*
Kapellmeister Kreisler came ever closer to destruction.
There was a tragic necessity about this, and the second
group of Kreisler fragments (in the second part of
Fantasiestücke) are pervaded with a corresponding aura
of intense tragic beauty. They were a fitting prelude to the
Kreisler fragments of *Kater Murr.*

The two outstanding ones were the *Musikalisch-
poetischer Klub* and the *Lehrbrief.* In both, signs of
Kreisler's growing insanity increased. In the *Klub,*
Kreisler's music is crippled by the lack of certain strings in
the upper register of the piano that he is supposed to play
at a social gathering. Thus he has a bass accompaniment,
but no treble. Kreisler substitutes a form of poetry, recited
in total darkness to the accompaniment of appropriate
chords which he plays on the strings that are left. The
recitation consists of an idyllic vision, a fantasy that be-

gins to fulfill all his desire for peace, harmony, beauty, freedom, and even for the beautiful girl who alone understands his "Geistersprache." This magnificent spell is broken by the vision of devilish monsters plaguing him, and he abruptly ends this bizarre musical-literary impromptu by cursing song and music. The lights are put on by someone who apparently senses the growing violence of Kreisler's madness.

The vision in *Ritter Gluck* provides an incisive commentary to this episode in Kreisler's life. It will be recalled that the process of entering fully into the world of music entailed crossing through the realm of dreams into truth, and that this realm was full of peril. Kreisler is here in danger of falling victim to this realm: the fearsome monsters, like those behind the ivory gate in Gluck's vision, threaten to destroy him before he has reached his goal. To be sure, Kreisler is then brought back to the actuality of the social gathering, but he is still preoccupied. He still yearns for freedom at the end of the fragment, for his fantasy still hovers in the endless spaces in the realm of dreams, wishing that he were a poor innocent melody, having escaped the demonry of the earth. " 'Fort muss ich bald auf irgend eine Weise.' Es geschah auch bald, wie er gesprochen." (I, 283.) Exactly how he "departed" is an open question. As far as Hoffmann himself was concerned, he probably was expressing the half-conscious wish to rid himself of his obsessive *alter ego*. As for Kreisler, it strongly suggests his ultimate insanity which was mentioned around this time in the *Brief an einen Freund*.

The haunting Kreisler image is exorcised in a whimsical manner in *Kreislers Lehrbrief*. Here Kreisler divides himself into two persons, a master and an apprentice musician, and writes an indenture to himself, as he sends himself out into the world. There is a sense of finality about this attempt by Hoffmann to purge himself of Kreisler, for it is at the end of the second part of the *Fantasiestücke*, with the approach of some kind of death for one of the Kreislers —indicated by a cross. The story contained in this fragment has mythical qualities. Its focal point is a magic stone of great beauty, surrounded by an aura of sublime music from which Chrysostomus, the main character, gains inspiration. This power in the stone stems from its being the site of the murder of a beautiful woman at the hands of a man of obscure origin who is dominated by demonic forces. This story has a pedagogical message for Kreisler, the apprentice, for it is "ein treffendes Bild . . . des irdischen Unterganges durch böses Wollen einer feindlichen Macht, dämonischer Missbrauch der Musik, aber dann Aufschwung zum Höheren, Verklärung in Ton und Gesang!" (I, 310.)

We have seen how Kreisler himself has been possessed by the Satanic powers acting in this story. In the *Musikalisch-poetischer Klub*, the frightening apparitions in his realm of dreams are envisaged as forms of Satan: "Freijäger —Konzertmeister—Wurmdoktor—*ricco mercante*. . . ." And he actually surrenders himself at one point: "Lass ab von mir!—ich will artig sein! ich will glauben, der Teufel sei ein *Galanthuomo* von den feinsten Sitten!"

It was the myths of Satan, demons, hell, and various kinds of underworlds that were preoccupying Hoffmann more and more at this stage of his career. His total state of mind is aptly symbolized by the figure of Kreisler at the *Musikalisch-poetischer Klub*, as he sits in the dark over a crippled musical instrument, accompanying himself on the low bass notes and groping in the endless regions of fantastic poetic dreams for a beautiful melody, but ending up again and again in some kind of hell.

The artist figure in Hoffmann's writings changed

abruptly after the above *Kreisleriana*. Kreisler all but disappeared from Hoffmann's writings for about five years, until the continuation of the Kreisler story in *Kater Murr*. In this interim there appeared a great variety of artist figures. In general, the change was manifested most dramatically in the appearance of the poet and painter as types of the Romantic artist, and a relative disregard for the musician.

At first, interest in the poet figure was closely associated with music. This is illustrated best by the dialog *Der Dichter und der Komponist*, in which the union of these two arts is discussed primarily with reference to the creation of operas. The personal implication here is obvious: it was the time of Hoffmann's collaboration with Fouqué on the opera *Undine*. The very title of *Kreislers musikalisch-poetischer Klub* attests further to the dual interest. The next step was to release the writer altogether from his connection with music. This had already happened temporarily in *Der goldne Topf*; and from the *Musikalisch-poetischer Klub* on, the writer generally was independent of other arts. With the possible exception of Anselmus in *Der goldne Topf*, however, the poet figure never reached the stature of a Kreisler or a Ritter Gluck.

Far more fully developed was the figure of the painter and allied artists (such as goldsmiths) who created for the visual sense. This character type emerged after Hoffmann had become accomplished and known as a writer, and added new features and dimensions to Hoffmann's literary art as a whole. The painter supplanted the musician in some important functions; there is even a striking counterpart to the musician (as represented by Ritter Gluck) in Berklinger, the painter in *Artushof*. The main result of this new interest for Hoffmann's writing was an adoption of some of the techniques and principles of the pictorial arts into literature. We have seen the visual concreteness and sensuality of Hoffmann's prose in *Ritter Gluck*. Now, in his last Berlin period, these qualities were distilled and crystallized in painters and their works, and in other ways became an even more predominant feature in his writing. He even formed a theory of literature from it, "das serapiontische Prinzip," which requires a clear inner visual faculty from the story-teller, and serves as an instrument for "painting" with words his romantic myths all the more colorfully.

The comparatively few musician figures in the works of this period demonstrate Hoffmann's marked loss of faith in the "other world" of music, to which Kreisler had been unswervingly devoted, in spite of the problems it caused him. Now there was much negative criticism, skepticism, even cynicism in Hoffmann's attitude toward musician figures. The serious story of the Moorish songstress, Zulema, in *Das Sanctus* is treated with almost hysterical buffoonery and destructive irony by its narrator and his audience. In *Rat Krespel* the main character rejoices in his freedom when his beautiful daughter, Antonie, dies, taking with her the most beautiful singing voice he knows, along with his favorite violin which is laid to rest with her. *Die Fermate* is the least negative, but somewhat restricted in scope: it ridicules both the German school of musical training and performance, based on the exacting and pedantic tyranny of the metronome to which Theodor is subjected; and also the Italian school represented by the relatively undisciplined extemporizing singers, Lauretta and Teresina. The ideal musician combines the two schools. Thus the story treats mainly matters of technique and style: the mythical world of music is absent. *Der*

Kampf der Sänger, one of Hoffmann's weaker stories, occasionally harks back to the Kreisler problems in its main character, Heinrich von Ofterdingen, but this musician figure is involved mainly in a series of events in which his love for Mathilde and his competition with the other minstrels are central. An exploration of music and the musician's roles is not the intent of the story. *Der Baron von B.* is the most cynical of Hoffmann's tales about musicians. The main character, although a very effective teacher of violin technique and also a revered patron of the arts, suffers from the pathological delusion that he is a consummate violinist. Scarcely a more grotesque situation could be imagined when this nobleman makes scratchy, wailing sounds on his instrument while imagining himself to be playing the music of the spheres. *Baron von B.* is the nadir of Hoffmann's negative attitude toward the musician. The upswing came only when Hoffmann returned to Kreisler in *Kater Murr.*

Meanwhile Hoffmann's major art was writing. In practicing it, however, he did not achieve any especially profound or original insights into its nature as he did with music and painting. Only in *Der goldne Topf* is there a writer as a main character in a major work. Yet even here, there is little of a specific nature relating exclusively to poetry. We are not told with certainty until the very end that Anselmus' appropriation of a realm in Atlantis is tantamount to his becoming a poet. He becomes a master figure in a cosmic myth without making an especially strong case for poetry as being the necessary instrument for acquiring the myth. Could not a musician or a painter conquer the same mythical realm through their respective arts?

His next poet figure of major importance after *Der*

goldne Topf is Nathanael in *Der Sandmann*. As with Anselmus, the art of writing does not have an especially distinctive role. Unlike Anselmus, Nathanael, as poet, is the instrument of the destructive rather than the creative forces of the mythical world. The poem that Nathanael writes in the story serves only to herald the annihilation of his and Klara's love through the Satanic magician, Coppelius (III, 38 f.). This poet, then, is condemned, partly through his art.

The only poet in Hoffmann's tales who begins to approach the stature of Anselmus is Balthasar in *Klein Zaches*. It should be noted, however, that Balthasar is *not* the central figure of the story, as is Anselmus, and the mythical world is not depicted as fully as in *Der goldne Topf*. Until the very end of *Klein Zaches*, attention is focused on the grotesque idol of a Philistine society that suppresses genuine poetry.

Of special interest as a figure joining the verbal and visual arts is the hermit Serapion, the hero of the title story in the collection *Die Serapionsbrüder*. It is easy to overlook the fact that Serapion was originally a poet, for it is not greatly emphasized, nor is the main problem of the story an artistic one. Serapion's delusion that he has been a martyr and lives in the Theban wastelands is not connected with the creation of a work of art, but is merely a vision of such reality for his inner life that no external facts can undermine it.

The reality of the inward faculty of seeing is the main point of the story in the context of the *Serapionsbrüder*. From it is derived the "serapiontisches Prinzip," expounded in the conversations of the brothers following this story, and also following *Rat Krespel*. This is the point in Hoffmann's career at which he is most keenly aware of exactly how the mind functions in a myth-creating Romantic author.

This mind is sharply dualistic with reference to the "internal" and "external" worlds, stemming from the premises of the "Duplizität des Seins." It is the internal mind which creates the poetic world and which must envisage its creations clearly in order to describe them fully. Thus Lothar believes: "Dein Einsiedler, mein Cyprianus, war ein wahrhafter Dichter, *er hatte das wirklich geschaut,* was er verkündete, und deshalb ergriff seine Rede Herz und Gemüt." (Italics mine.) The role of the external world is that of a stimulus: ". . . es ist unser irdisches Erbteil, dass eben die Aussenwelt, in der wir eingeschachtet, als der Hebel wirkt, der jene Kraft in Bewegung setzt." This all applies to Serapion and his insane, though poetic visions, therefore he is chosen as the ideal narrator for the brothers to emulate (V, 94 f.).

Lest the "Serapionsbrüder" themselves be regarded as insane, however, an important distinction is made between Serapion and other poets: Serapion is totally unaware of the external stimulus of internal poetic creation: "Aber du, o mein Einsiedler, statuiertest keine Aussenwelt, du sahst den versteckten Hebel nicht, die auf dein Inneres einwirkende Kraft. . . ." Thus no matter how fantastic a "Serapiontic" story may become, its point of departure must be in actual experience.

The inner vision, then, becomes part of actuality, for the brothers decide that it is the goal of each narrator, "das Bild, das ihm im Innern aufgegangen, recht zu erfassen mit allen seinen Gestalten, Farben, Lichtern und Schatten und dann, wenn er sich recht entzündet davon fühlt, *die Darstellung ins äussere Leben zu tragen*" (italics mine). Thus the fantastic image is fused with actuality both in its origin and in its final, concrete form. This is done primarily through the sense of seeing.

This was nothing new in Hoffmann's literary career, but was rather a verbalization of a theory that he had been practicing since *Ritter Gluck*. Is not Gluck's vision "Serapiontic" in all senses—in the visual quality, the origin in actuality, and the final concrete form—and is not Hoffmann's depiction thereof likewise in complete accordance with these criteria? One could apply this to almost all of Hoffmann's works, but it is especially valid for the mythical ones, in which highly fantastic elements become more fantastic because they are so life-like, are "borne into actuality," and comprise then a part of the cosmos. Thus the Serapiontic principle is a major factor in the unity of Hoffmann's whole literary accomplishment. In spite of the great variety of themes and plots, the same fundamental principle of "envisionment," along with the same mythical world, underlie his stories.

The growing awareness of the pictorial nature of his writing was accompanied by increased use of the motifs related to the art of painting. It is no accident that the very next story after the above discussion in the *Serapionsbrüder—Die Fermate*—uses a vividly described painting as a point of departure, and that the visual arts have a predominant role in the period during which the stories of this collection were written.

The partial displacement of music by painting in Hoffmann's writings is most dramatically illustrated by *Der Artushof*, which constitutes a pictorial counterpart to the musical *Ritter Gluck*. As the latter was written at the beginning of Hoffmann's interest in music as a literary theme (1808), so was *Der Artushof* written around the inception of his rapidly increasing attention as a writer to painting (1815). Certain basic elements are common to both stories. The nature of the art involved is revealed by an older man (Gottfried Berklinger) to a younger one (Traugott) who becomes a kind of disciple. There is an aura of the supernatural and miraculous about both Gluck and Berklinger; in fact, both are revenants of a former age: Gluck from the eighteenth, Berklinger from the fifteenth century. Most striking of all is that the master works of both are represented by blank surfaces: Gluck's by unused note paper, Berklinger's by an unpainted canvas.

In *Der Artushof,* however, there is nothing resembling the extensive myth of the artist's world in *Ritter Gluck.* Instead, the blank canvas is briefly described (V, 185 f.) as an idyllic nature myth very similar to the description of Atlantis in *Der goldne Topf.* This brevity apparently stems from the intention that prevails in most of Hoffmann's artist stories: to portray the artist type and his problems per se, rather than delve extensively into the subject matter of his art.

An element in the painter story that is not present in *Ritter Gluck* is the figure of the idealized woman who embodies a personal myth, represented here by Felizitas, a parallel figure to Kreisler's Julia. Felizitas' appeal lies in Traugott's conviction that she is the "beloved of his soul," whom he has always known and occasionally seen in dreams without having met her. Her role in his life is to inspire his art. Marriage with her, however, is out of the question. Traugott can hope for marriage only with Felizitas' "earthly" counterpart, Dorina. Behind these events lies Hoffmann's growing conviction that the artist frequently experiences a special kind of love for women, and that this love remains productive for him as an artist only if it remains purely artistic, i.e., a haunting vision, unattained except through art, and often originating from a myth, like Serpentina.

This conviction is even more poignantly illustrated by Hoffmann's next story about a painter, *Die Jesuiterkirche in G.*, telling of the torments of Berthold, a half-insane genius whose tragedy lies in his inability to combine normal and artistic love in his relationship with his wife. By marrying his ideal beloved, who, as Hoffmann believes, should remain in the realm of the artist's myth, he defiles "die Liebe des Künstlers," which Hoffmann later discusses at length in *Kater Murr* (IX, 143 ff.). As in *Der Artushof,* the face of the beloved first appears to Berthold in a painting, evoking a haunting reminiscence of his dreams of ideal beauty.

Still another type of myth appears in this story: that of landscapes. It is, to be sure, an embryonic one, for Hoffmann was no great lover of nature as were some English Romanticists such as Wordsworth. He nonetheless seeks a myth in the natural phenomena of a landscape, and succeeds in creating one in the abstract. This occurs when Berthold, in his struggle to find the right genre of painting for his abilities, turns away from realistic landscape scenes to more fantastic ones, in which the essence of the landscape is portrayed, rather than external appearances. A mysterious figure, the Maltese gentleman who is reminiscent of Gluck and Berklinger, is instrumental in this experiment. He, too, seems to be from a different world, which Berthold seeks in nature. Berthold does not master this genre, however. The only genuinely concrete and intense figure from this world who takes on reality is the ideal feminine figure whom Berthold envisages while painting at the grotto scene in Naples (III, 115 f.). She then becomes a central image in his mind, around which all else revolves.

Otherwise the nature myth is presented merely in the abstract: "Der Geweihte vernimmt die Stimme der Natur, die in wunderbaren Lauten aus Baum, Gebüsch, Blume, Berg und Gewässer von unerforschlichem Geheimnis spricht, die in seiner Brust sich zu frommer Ahnung gestalten; dann kommt, wie der Geist Gottes selbst, die Gabe über ihn, diese Ahnung sichtlich in seine Werke zu übertragen." When Berthold contemplates the paintings of the masters, the Maltese gentleman claims: " . . . der Geist, der aus dem Ganzen wehte, hob dich empor in ein höheres Reich, dessen Abglanz du zu schauen wähntest . . . Bist du eingedrungen in den tiefern Sinn der Natur, so werden selbst in deinem Innern ihre Bilder in hoher glänzender Pracht aufgehen." (III, 113.) It would be possible to transform this into a genuine literary nature myth resembling that of Phillip Otto Runge in his painting, *Der Morgen*. This does not come about, however. Berthold's *magnum opus* turns out ultimately to be in a conventional genre and style. It is, to be sure, pervaded with the aura of the higher realm as manifested in nature. This realm is not represented in characteristic images, however, as in Hoffmann's greater literary accomplishments; we are merely assured that it is there.

Der Artushof and *Die Jesuiterkirche* are sufficient as illustrations of the main themes related to Hoffmann's painter figures. A few details in later works show some further development of these themes. Other visual arts— those of the goldsmith and the maker of fine barrels—are used with great vividness and meaning in *Das Fräulein von Scuderi* and *Meister Martin der Küfner und seine Gesellen*, respectively. In the first, Cardillac's art is especially appropriate to his character due to the association of gold with its subterranean origins in the realm of demons. Meister Martin's art of barrelmaking has the down-to-earth qualities associated with the milieu of the burghers of sixteenth-century Nuremburg. Some sophistication is injected, however, in that one of his journeymen is a nobleman, another a painter, the third a goldsmith. The great past of Nuremberg and vicinity, with its cultivation of the visual arts and crafts, becomes a highly appropriate background for two other stories: *Meister Johannes Wacht* and *Der Feind*. The latter, its main character being Albrecht Dürer, could well have been one of Hoffmann's most powerful works, had his death not prevented its completion.

The most significant new possibility for Hoffmann's mythical world in the painter stories was, however, the nature myth, and this did not really mature. Only in *Signor Formica* is its theory carried a step beyond *Die Jesuiterkirche*—but only a step, in that it is somewhat more fully discussed in the abstract. In this long-winded, but amusing potboiler, there is much serious and worthwhile discussion of art in the conversations between Salvator Rosa *alias* Signor Formica and his disciple, Antonio Scacciati. The type of painting mentioned most often is the same peculiar fantastic genre of the landscape scenes as that referred to in *Die Jesuiterkirche in G.*:

Es ist die oft übermenschliche Grösse der Gedanken, die ich in Euren Werken anstaune. Ihr erfasst die tiefsten Geheimnisse der Natur, Ihr erschaut die wunderbaren Hieroglyphen ihrer Felsen, ihrer Bäume, ihrer Wasserfälle, Ihr vernehmt ihre heilige Stimme, Ihr versteht ihre Sprache und habt die Macht, es aufzuschreiben, was sie zu Euch gesprochen.—Ja, ein *Aufschreiben* möcht' ich Euer keckes, kühnes Malen nennen

. . . Scheint oft dieser, jener Felsen, dieser, jener Baum wie ein riesiger Mensch mit ernstem Blick uns anzuschauen, so gleicht diese, jene Gruppe seltsam gekleideter Menschen wiederum einem wunderbaren, lebendig gewordnen Gestein. . . . (VIII, 28 f.)

The idea of such an "Aufschreiben" of nature apparently came from Hoffmann's preoccupation with landscape painting. Although, as indicated, he was not the author to do this to the fullest possible extent, there are in his later works some myths at least related to his ideal of fantastic landscape painting. The main examples (to be discussed in detail later) are: *Das fremde Kind* (the forest), *Die Bergwerke zu Falun* (the subterranean regions), and *Die Königsbraut* (a village garden). Hoffmann was apparently too much a man of the city to form a myth of the countryside into a single, coherent whole. Besides, the cosmic myth that accompanied him most of his life transcended and included these myths.

The three categories of the artist in Hoffmann's tales illustrate in great variety the problems of the Romantic artist, the instrument of Romantic myth. In these stories the myth itself is not revealed so much as is the type of person preoccupied with it. They contribute, however, to our understanding of Hoffmann's methods and means of representing the mythical world. The musician offers harmony, thematic composition, and a pure, non-representational art; the painter provides visual concreteness and a whole literary theory associated therewith, "das serapiontische Prinzip"; the writer adopts and utilizes what he can from the others, and in the conviction of the fundamental reality of the demonic and higher *Märchen* worlds, explores and reveals them.

5

Tales of the Satanic

We have seen several satanic figures in the works already
discussed. In *Ritter Gluck* the composer's realm of dreams
was inhabited by frightening monsters. In *Der goldne
Topf*, there was the witch-figure, Liese, surrounded by
various types of hellish creatures; furthermore, her origin
from a beet-root and a black dragon feather suggests
thematically a mythical fountainhead for the whole satanic
clan and underworld realm subsequently created in Hoffmann's tales. In the Kreisler fragments we saw the poet-
musician obsessed by Satan himself. Now, from 1814 to
1817, we see Hoffmann increasingly haunted by satanic
figures of various kinds. This came about, strangely
enough, during a time in his life when he was enjoying an
ever-increasing professional and social security. There appears to be little external cause for the anxieties and depressions that are so characteristic of these devil-ridden
tales. It is the opposite condition from that under which
he wrote *Der goldne Topf*, the work in which he created

an internal security of a primeval world of art in which all his frustrated aspirations in a hostile world seemed fulfilled. Now in more prosperous circumstances, he needed to explore the depth of his own personal hell and the tormenting figures inhabiting it.

Hoffmann's underworld is not clearly circumscribed and organized. It is definitely to be contrasted with the upper regions of his primeval world, a kind of Paradise. Hoffmann's hell does not lend itself to clear analysis, for it is a black, bottomless abyss, containing a negative principle manifesting itself irrationally in blind destruction of creativity. This often comes about in scenes in which satanic figures emerge suddenly out of darkness, as when in *Ignaz Denner* the brigands and their leader suddenly come out of a pitch-black forest to destroy a virtuous life. The entire underworld will be discussed in the next chapter, for it involves matters extending beyond satanic figures. This chapter will be devoted to figures modeled more or less on the traditional image of Satan.

The outstanding work of this period is *Die Elixiere des Teufels*. The very title indicates the role played by Satan, for the novel is pervaded by an atmosphere originating, so to speak, from the fumes generated by a bottle of elixirs—a relic—with which Satan once tried to tempt St. Anthony. Satan himself does not appear in his traditional form, but the story is dominated by his aura, and manipulated by his agents.

The main action of the story is initiated, symbolically, by a plunge into the depths. This occurs when Medardus, a monk on his first excursion into the world, unintentionally causes his lascivious and murderous half-brother to fall into an abyss. Previous to this there have been strong symptoms of Medardus' potential sinfulness, but it is through this event that the potentiality is activated. A hollow voice—that of the man in the abyss—speaks out of the depths of Medardus' unknown *alter ego*, and now the whole monstrous burden of his ancestors' guilt wells up in him.

Well over half of the novel resembles pieces of a jigsaw puzzle spread out haphazardly among a series of seemingly unrelated episodes. Medardus' strange childhood and early career as a monk; his instinctive love for Aurelie; his sinful liaison with Euphemie and the murder of Hermogen at the Baron von F.'s castle; the stern admonitions of "der alte Maler" at the "Handelsstadt"; the frightening visit to the forester's lodge, where Viktorin, his "double," haunts him; his arrest, release, love affair, and near marriage with Aurelie when he plays the role of Leonard Krczynski von Kwiecziczewo at the palace of Fürst von W.; his stay at the Italian insane asylum—these events and many more seem to contain fragments of a picture, the totality of which is vaguely sensed but not envisaged completely until Medardus is granted a revelation. This comes about when he reads a manuscript giving a cryptic history of the previous five generations of his family. When diagrammed,[1] the family tree resembles the rampant growth of a parasitic plant as described by Hoffmann himself in the foreword: "Du erkennst den verborgenen Keim, den ein dunkles Verhängnis gebar, und der, zur üppigen Pflanze emporgeschossen, fort und fort wuchert, in tausend Ranken, bis *eine* Blüte, zur Frucht reifend, allen Lebenssaft an sich zieht und den Keim selbst tötet." (II, 22.) The enlightenment gained from the manuscript leads to Medardus' even-

[1] See my diagram and interpretation thereof in "The Family Tree in E. T. A. Hoffmann's *Die Elixiere des Teufels*," *PMLA*, LXXIII (1958), 516-520.

tual repentance and penance, and his chances for ultimate salvation.

Although this background story is not a myth itself, it nonetheless employs techniques similar to those used with several genuine myths in other stories. These arise from a similar over-all structure, for in both *Die Elixiere des Teufels* and the genuinely mythical tales a large and coherent body of information lurks under the surface of the events portrayed, is frequently alluded to in a mysterious manner, and is brought to light in some kind of revelation.

Lurking in the background of *Die Elixiere des Teufels* there is a type of myth in the legend of St. Anthony and the Devil (II, 37 ff.). This is an *Urbild* of Medardus' life, who even claims to be St. Anthony at one point. The episode in this legend that is most relevant to Medardus is that in which Satan tempts St. Anthony with the bottle of elixirs, which is possessed by the monastery as a relic and is drunk by Medardus. Another parallel is Satan's appearance as a bedraggled beggar—the form later taken by Viktorin, and also Medardus when he is most closely identical with Viktorin.

Harking back to the background myth while reading the story gives us a clearer awareness of the exact role of the satanic figures in the novel—namely, that of tempter. Viktorin is not Satan himself, but he resembles him externally and also epitomizes the lascivious and murderous tendencies of Medardus' family, thus being an instrument serving Satan's purposes. The externally generated guilt is then made internal when Viktorin's character seems to enter Medardus. Thus a man—a monk, who more than anyone is expected to approach spiritual and moral perfection—is subverted by satanic forces.

Here, as in *Der goldne Topf*, a human being's ostensible

character is shaken to its foundation, and brought to a necessary natural development that before has been scarcely manifested. Just as poetic forces "break through" into Anselmus' life, in like manner satanic might emerges violently in Medardus. In this case, however, the myth embodies forces which are more clearly "internal"—i.e., psychological. From this point of view, the satanic Viktorin is merely a piece of Medardus' own character. The myth here becomes an inherent part of the psyche. Such considerations are the foundation for the interest taken by C. G. Jung and his disciples in Hoffmann's psychologically symbolic figures and motifs which they regard as archetypal images.[2] For the individual's life they provide "die symbolische Erkenntnis des geheimen Fadens . . . der sich durch unser Leben zieht, es festknüpfend in allen seinen Bedingungen . . ." (II, 22.)

Satanic motifs are, of course, a part of the whole Christian literary tradition, which by mere association must be indicated by the novel's main themes. Such things as monastic life, a concept of saintliness (Aurelie and the Abbess), the original sin (in the discussion with the Pope, II, 235 f.) and the liturgy appear in obvious connections with beliefs including satanic forms of evil. Such motifs as these—relating to the church as the Devil's adversary—hardly match the satanic ones in interest and originality, and are not mythical. The devilish Euphemie and Viktorin are likely to make a far more vivid impression than the saintly Aurelie and the repentant, crusading Hermogen.

Thus in Hoffmann's second major work he went into the opposite direction from that of *Der goldne Topf*. From

[2] The most extensive Jungian study of Hoffmann is Aniela Jaffé's *Bilder und Symbole aus E. T. A. Hoffmanns Märchen "Der goldne Topf,"* in *Gestaltungen des Unbewussten*, VII (Zürich, 1950).

the sublimity of the poetic realm of Atlantis at the end of *Der goldne Topf,* Hoffmann plunged almost immediately into the chasms of *Die Elixiere des Teufels.* According to his diary, he finished *Der goldne Topf* on February 15, 1814, and began *Die Elixiere* on March 5. And there were soon even more devils to come. The main ones were those in the shorter stories *Ignaz Denner, Die Abentheuer der Silvesternacht,* and *Der Sandmann.*

The writing of *Ignaz Denner* ran from the spring of 1814 (entitled at first *Der Revierjäger*) into 1816 when it underwent final revision. These were the first two years of Hoffmann's demonic period, and this work is basic to its understanding, although as a whole the plot of the story does not permit its inclusion among Hoffmann's best. The main character, Ignaz Denner, and his father, Doctor Trabacchio, are in league with Satan. Their principal role in the story is to tempt Andres, a morally impeccable man, to commit evil by collaborating with their band of brigands engaged in theft, plunder, and murder. Andres' torture of conscience is matched only by Medardus'. The atmosphere of the story is set by the empty blackness of a forest at night from which frightening figures, like apparitions, suddenly emerge. When Andres is taken to the band of brigands for the first time, it is like an intense picture of the very Cocytus of Hoffmann's personal hell: "überall in den Büschen flackerten Windlichter auf, und es rauschte und klirrte in den dunklen Gängen, bis sich schwarze grässliche Gestalten gespenstisch hervordrängten und den Denner im Kreise umringten." (III, 65.) Andres' forced participation in the band's crimes, his indictment, and ultimate chance for salvation are generally parallel to the story of Medardus.

There are important differences from the *Elixiere,* however. First, there is no background myth comparable to the legend of St. Anthony. Instead, only the traditional features and roles of Satan form the motivating forces underlying the tale. There is, however, a background story involving previous generations in the revelation of Denner's and Trabacchio's pact with the devil and practice of black magic.

It is the motifs of black magic which distinguish this demonic background most from the *Elixiere*. An evil master figure—first Trabacchio, then Denner—is central to this realm. The demonry emanating from them is driven to a fantastic extreme, with the seduction and murder of young women, the dissection of children's bodies, and the almost limitless magic powers enabling Trabacchio even to escape from execution. He is one of several demonic magicians appearing in this phase of Hoffmann's writings.

There is another important difference between the two works. It will be remembered that all the forces motivating *Die Elixiere des Teufels* originate or are represented in Medardus himself, and are therefore in large measure of a psychological nature. This is not true of Andres, for he is in all respects a paragon of virtue. Even the universal guilt which is part of his devoutly practiced creed is scarcely visible in him. The idea of such guilt is, of course, basic to *Die Elixiere des Teufels*. In *Ignaz Denner*, satanic forces are projected onto figures and milieus that are beyond common human experience—onto a learned doctor from a distant land, whose agents operate in a black and sinister German forest.

Die Abentheuer der Silvesternacht also employs a nocturnal background, as indicated by the title. It is the last complete story in the second volume of *Phantasiestücke in Callots Manier*, but belongs to a different phase of

Hoffmann's writings from that of the other stories in the collection. It was written after *Der Revierjäger*, and could well have been included in the *Nachtstücke* of 1817. In it Hoffmann continued to objectify his innermost anxieties and depressions, this time, however, through "Doppelgänger" figures. The story is told by a "travelling enthusiast," from whom we are slightly alienated by an implicit irony. Further narrative alienation takes place when the central episode (Chapter IV) is told within the frame of the "enthusiast's" story.

This chapter, "Die Geschichte vom verlornen Spiegelbild," is an obvious variation on several themes from Chamisso's *Peter Schlemihl*, the hero of which actually appears earlier in the story. The lost mirror image corresponds to Peter's shadow, Giulietta to Mina, Dapertutto to the "gray gentleman," and Erasmus' uncertain wandering fate to Peter's after he has acquired his seven league boots. The connection with Satan is suggested by an exchange agreement, common to both stories and similar to Faust's pact with Mephisto. As in *Peter Schlemihl*, the sinner loses, instead of his soul, something symbolizing that part of his personality on which his social acceptability is based.

Nonetheless there is much that is more typical of Hoffmann than of Chamisso in the story. Especially Hoffmannesque are Giulietta and Dapertutto, who wield a sinister influence over Spikher in their roles as tempters. Giulietta is related to Hoffmann's Julia, the "Geliebte der Seele." She is her demonic variation, however, in her role as a seductive courtesan, trying to persuade Spikher, a virtuous husband and father, to murder his family in order to devote himself completely to her. Likewise Dapertutto is a typically Hoffmannesque satanic figure, who by comparison makes the devil in Schlemihl appear a pale gray indeed! Dapertutto (which means "Everywhere") proves the appropriateness of his name by attempting—in league with Giulietta—to influence Spikher wherever he goes in Italy and Germany, once he has been tempted by Giulietta. Also, Dapertutto possesses skill in the occult sciences.

As with Medardus and Andres, the satanic figure ultimately fails. Spikher is left wandering, however, without any suggestion of the eventual consolation and salvation achieved by Medardus and Andres. *Die Abenteuer der Silvesternacht* is, then, a further development of Hoffmann's satanic figures in the strong suggestion of Dapertutto's identity as Satan himself, in the role of procurer for a courtesan of overpowering seductiveness, and in objectivizing the problem by creating a "Doppelgänger." These elements in themselves are not new, but in combination provide one of Hoffmann's more successful demonic tales.

Der Sandmann presents the high point of the power and fearsomeness of a satanic figure in the demonic tales. This is made all the more impressive by an ingenious and subtle development of motifs throughout the story. The course of the tale leads Nathanael inexorably to destruction at the hands of a hostile force, which is embodied again in a satanic "Wunderdoktor," Coppelius *alias* Coppola, who possesses magical powers (like Trabacchio and Dapertutto). The whole web of circumstances surrounding him is masterfully woven together by thematic association, having its origin in a short, but effective background story consisting of motifs of a *Märchenmythos*. This is the gruesome "fairy tale" about the "Sandmann" told to Nathanael as a child by an old nursemaid: "Das ist ein böser Mann, der kommt zu den Kindern, wenn sie nicht zu Bett gehen wollen, und wirft ihnen Hände voll Sand in die Augen, dass sie blutig zum Kopf herausspringen, die wirft er dann in den Sack und trägt sie in den Halbmond zur Atzung für seine Kinderchen; die sitzen dort im Nest und haben krumme Schnäbel, wie die Eulen, damit picken sie der unartigen Menschenkindlein Augen auf." (III, 24 f.) The folk-tale quality here is obvious. Also the fact that it is a fairy tale, told to a child, is significant in its anticipation of Hoffmann's later children's fairy tales. For *Der Sandmann* itself the passage is an initial focal point from which the main action in the remainder of the tale is generated— a technique that we have observed in *Der goldne Topf*.

The first thematic association with this tale appears in Coppelius, a sinister, ugly old man whom children instinctively fear and identify with the "Sandmann." Then in the nightmarish scene in the alchemistic laboratory, the eyes motif is further developed when Coppelius sadistically threatens to remove Nathanael's eyes. Then, when Coppelius returns in the form of the Italian, Coppola, he is again occupied with "eyes" in the form of optical instruments. The dénouement of the Olimpia story comes when Coppelius demands the return of her eyes. Finally it is one of Coppelius' "eyes" (a telescope) that sets off Nathanael's final attack of insanity when he views Klara through it, mistakes her for Olimpia, tries to murder her, then commits suicide. Thus the story evolves out of a fanciful background tale by thematic association, as in *Der goldne Topf*. In *Der Sandmann*, however, the structure is far less complex, for there is only the one predominant theme of eyes, and the plot follows a more or less straight line of development with simple variations on it. *Der goldne Topf* is infinitely more complex in its organically burgeoning themes and variations.

One aspect of the work sets it apart from most of Hoffmann's other fantastic tales. This is the shaky ground of reality on which the fantastic elements rest. The objective validity of the fantastic world is highly suspect here as nowhere else in Hoffmann's tales. The background tale is an obvious fabrication by a very unwise old nursemaid who clumsily—and perhaps sadistically—tries to frighten her charges into being good little children. She is hardly trying to reveal cosmic truths to devoted disciples, as elsewhere in Hoffmann's mythical tales. The scene in the father's laboratory has all the earmarks of a bad dream, including Nathanael's waking up in the morning, surprised at being in his own bed, and not in the laboratory. As the story progresses into the most fantastic part of all—Nathanael's love for an automaton—the actuality of Nathanael's personal experiences becomes increasingly doubtful, especially with Klara's admonitions to turn his mind away from his supposed mysterious enemy. Merely by doing this, she claims, he can eradicate Coppelius' influence (III, 37).

In this story, then, Hoffmann is challenging the reality of an area of his world of fantasy, which previously he had often considered to be more real than the humdrum world of everyday. Not only is their reality challenged, but all other possible usefulness and validity in them. Nathanael is obviously destroyed by creations of his imagination. It is possible, in a general sense, that he is overcome by an evil *power* that one could call "satanic." But the satanic *figure* as such is fully real only to him.

If Nathanael's fantastic world does not represent the unseen foundation of actuality, as elsewhere in Hoffmann's works, what is it? The most strongly suggested alternative is a psychological symbolism. Nathanael shows a thinly

veiled infantile tendency in his attraction toward an over-
grown toy (Olimpia), in his capricious behavior toward
Klara and Lothar, and—most of all—in his anxieties stemming from a fairy tale and a bad dream. Psychologically,
then, his fantastic visions are distortions imposed on reality
and stemming from a child's point of view that has become seriously warped. Especially strong evidence for this
psychological level is the scene where Nathanael looks at
Klara through Coppelius' telescope and sees Olimpia.
Thus, thinking back on the story, Olimpia turns out to be
a fantastic projection of Klara into Nathanael's anxiety-
ridden mind. What appears to be Satan in league with a
woman and an evil "Wunderdoktor" turns out to be a
childish misogyny and fear of a father figure.

In the context of Hoffmann's career as a writer and man,
this story has its positive value, for it shows his clear
awareness of the dangers of his fantastic world, along with
a vision of better things to come. The meaningful touch
at the end—Klara's happy marriage—should be regarded
in this light. The extreme satanic depths of mood antici-
pate an ascension into the light—a course which Hoffmann
indicated in *Kreislers Lehrbrief* in musical terms during
the same year in which he wrote *Der Sandmann*. Thus the
story can be seen as: "ein treffendes Bild . . . des irdischen
Unterganges durch böses Wollen einer feindlichen Macht,
dämonischer Missbrauch der Musik [in this case 'der
Dichtung'], aber dann Aufschwung zum Höheren, Verklärung in Ton und Gesang." (I, 310.)

A new variety of devil then emerged—one who was far
easier to cope with. This is epitomized by the "hero" of
Nachricht aus dem Leben eines bekannten Mannes, a
fantastic anecdote in the *Serapionsbrüder*, having its
source in a sixteenth-century chronicle. The remoteness

in time from Hoffmann's era is significant: Satan is here safely relegated to a time when people still believed in him—the implication being that Hoffmann does not. The form taken by the "well-known man" on his visitation to Berlin is anything but sinister: he is a good-natured and well-liked burgher who on the surface possesses all the conventional middle-class virtues, with only occasional eccentric behavior associated with his limp. In fact, his identity might never have come out in the story had it not been for Barbara Roloffin, the old woman servant who is really a witch and causes her employer's wife to bear a grotesque monster instead of a child. In order to rescue her from the stake it is necessary for him to transform himself into a giant bat, and pull her out of the flames. Even this sinister form, however, cannot completely erase the affable image of him that we have from the beginning.

Lothar, the fictitious author of the story in the *Serapionsbrüder*, rebukes Theodor for having brought a copy of this story to their gathering, and firmly denounces it in the conversations before and after the reading. This attitude is an accurate reflection of Hoffmann's growing distaste for devils. If there are to be any, then let them be, it is suggested (VII, 22), *German* devils—not, presumably, the kind imported from Italy, such as Trabacchio, Dapertutto, and Coppola. The native variety, although still an evil tempter, is at least "gemütlich," conscientious, and punctual. He does, it is true, allow himself to be outwitted occasionally, and has an unpleasantly burlesque side, but this does not matter much. Furthermore, opposition is expressed here to giving Satan any qualities that go to extremes, such as is found in literature of that day: "Entweder wird der Teufel zum gemeinen Hanswurst,

oder das Grauenhafte, Unheimliche zerreisst das Gemüt."
This is a far cry from *Die Elixiere des Teufels!*

Lothar sums up Hoffmann's new literary devil: "genug,
die Sache bleibt für uns rein phantastisch, und selbst das
unheimliche Spukhafte, das sonst dem 'furchtbar vernein-
enden Prinzip der Schöpfung' beiwohnt, kann, durch den
komischen Kontrast, in dem es erscheint, nur jenes seltsame Gefühl hervorbringen, das, eine eigentümliche Mischung des Grauenhaften und Ironischen, uns auf gar nicht
unangenehme Weise spannt." (VII, 19.) With this the
demonry in the story is not completely dissipated, for
Lothar goes on to say that the horror of the witch's story
in the *Nachricht aus dem Leben eines bekannten Mannes*
affected him deeply.

In spite of this final serious touch, the story as a whole
illustrates the decrease in Hoffmann's obsession with
satanic figures. This does not mean that he ceased to peer
with fascination into a dark chaos, teeming with frightening grotesque figures. Quite the contrary. But it was this
whole underworld into which he was increasingly delving
during the vacillations of his fantasy.

6

The Underworld

The figures emerging from the black chaos in several of Hoffmann's tales are many and various. Beginning primarily as variations on Satan, they are then transformed into many types representing the forces of darkness and destruction. The all-embracing symbol for this realm is the night. This is reflected in the very title of the key work of this phase, *Nachtstücke*.

Hoffmann experimented with various forms of his underworld. Consequently there were varying degrees of success in creating the appropriate means of expression. He himself recognized this unevenness in *Nachtstücke* when he wrote in his letter of March 8, 1818, to Kunz: "Im zweiten Theil der Nachtstücke empfehle ich Ihnen das Majorat und das Gelübde; das öde Haus taugt nichts und das steinerne Herz ist so—so!"

The first two stories in the collection—*Der Sandmann* (1815) and *Ignaz Denner* (1814-1816)—actually belong more to the earlier "satanic" phase of Hoffmann's writings than the others, and were therefore discussed in detail in the previous chapter. Associated with these satanic figures there is, of course, an "underworld." In the first, the symbolic night atmosphere is the backdrop for the activities of a practitioner of black magic, who evokes tormenting anxieties in children, creates the beautiful, but deceptive figure of superhuman beauty (Olimpia), and drives Nathanael to madness. At the same time, it is an exploration of the abyss of a mind which creates for itself such fearsome creatures and situations. In *Ignaz Denner,* the underworld is a sinister forest, in which thieves and murderers have their refuge and base of operation, and infect others with brutality and baseness. In both cases the underworld night atmosphere clearly exists in actuality, and therefore is not in itself mythical; it is, however, pervaded with a power derived from a satanic concept, and is therefore strongly suggestive of a myth.

In *Die Jesuiterkirche in G.* Hoffmann greatly extended his exploration of that part of the underworld involving mainly the artist, in this case Berthold, a painter who in his absolute devotion to his art is on the verge of criminal insanity. (A discussion of this artistic aspect of the story appears in Chapter III.) There is a strong demonic element in Berthold's art. This comes up in connection with the nature myth, which apparently also includes a threatening underworld: "Die ganze Natur, ihm sonst freundlich lächelnd, ward ihm zum bedrohlichen Ungeheuer, und ihre Stimme, die sonst in des Abendwindes Säuseln, in dem Plätschern des Baches, in dem Rauschen des Gebüsches mit süssem Wort ihn begrüsste, verkündete ihm nun Untergang und Verderben." (III, 114.) One might expect Hoffmann to portray these "threatening monsters" in some concrete form or other, but this would probably have tended to shift the center of attention from the artist figure per se. Thus in *Die Jesuiterkirche in G.*, he did not develop any further a demonic world of nature in landscapes, just as he had left a *Märchen* landscape-myth in embryonic form.

Das Sanctus, the final story of the first volume of *Nachtstücke*, adds but little to Hoffmann's underworld. The tale provides a capriccio-like ending to this otherwise bleak collection; for an extreme tone of irony, even buffoonery, is created by the narrators and audience in the *Rahmen*. The bearing of *Das Sanctus* on the night and underworld symbolism lies in its preoccupation with mental illness—a mild kind, to be sure: a psychological block preventing a singer from performing. The source of this aspect of the "Nachtseite" of life is clearly G. H. von Schubert's *Ansichten von der Nachtseite der Naturwissenschaften* and similar works. One of the comments of the doctor to the narrator abounds with typical terms from Schubert: " 'O,' rief der Doktor lachend, 'o, nur Geduld, er wird gleich auf seinem Steckenpferde sitzen und gestreckten Galopps in die Welt der Ahnungen, Träume, psychischen Einflüsse, Sympathien, Idiosynkrasien u. s. w. hineinreiten, bis er auf der Station des Magnetismus absitzt und ein Frühstück nimmt.' " (III, 125.) It is obvious that the area of the underworld discussed is not especially fearsome in this case, nor even to be taken seriously. Even the deep earnestness of the inner story of Zulema, the Moorish convert to Christianity, is attenuated by its remoteness in time and place from the narrative present, and by the buffoonery of the dialogue surrounding it.

Such a mechanism of irony could not operate, however, in *Das öde Haus*, the first story in the second volume of *Nachtstücke*. Something is definitely lacking that might possibly have resolved the dilemma of the two mutually incompatible realities presented in this story. Irony could not be the solution here, however, for Theodor, the narrator and hero, is too desperate to laugh in his vain search for deeper forces underlying everyday life—which are embodied in myth in other tales of Hoffmann. Thus the story is, in a sense, incomplete; this might have been what Hoffmann sensed about it when he called it "worthless." One might be inclined to agree with him, were it not for certain aspects of it, making it important in the development of his demonic tales. Few stories by him are so weak as a whole but so interesting in individual parts.

The desolate house stands at the center of attention as an appropriate symbol of wearisome emptiness and decay that cries out for identity and vitality. Theodor feels this intensely as he walks by it, for he can identify it with his own need for something to deepen and nurture his insights into his own everyday life. Theodor is absolutely opposed to "prosaic" solutions to important problems. This word "prosaic" recurs several times in the story; then he attaches it as attributive to a "demon" plaguing him with rational explanations for the mysteries that he wants to see (III, 142 f.).

Thus when he sees the portrait of a beautiful woman— an ideal feminine figure—in the window, he endows it with a life stemming from his most desperate need for some spiritual regeneration. The way is paved thereby for a breakthrough of a myth embodying the transcendent powers for which he seems to be yearning. Another Anselmus is in the making.

Nothing of the kind comes about, however. The remainder of the story is a confused jumble of explanations, counter-explanations, mysteries, and frustrations. As in

Der Sandmann, great suspicion is cast on the hero's sanity. Here he even goes to a psychiatrist! Unlike the story of Nathanael, however, there is no tragic resolution of the problem. Theodor is *not* necessarily insane. After all, even the psychiatrist sees the image of the ideal beloved in the "magic mirror." Moreover, if Theodor is insane, then he has a chance of entering into long-distant spiritual rapport with various strange beings by means of the occult powers with which the mentally ill are believed to be endowed. This association is supported by the neurotic Edwine, who is the realization of Theodor's image of the ideal beloved, and is somehow shown to be in communication with the powers controlling the mysteries in the tale.

Then we have the "rational" explanation for it all in a background story of the previous generation. Jealousy, adultery, child-stealing, and revenge make up a fitting backdrop for the ominous "desolate house." Behind it all, in turn, stands a mysterious old woman and her gypsy band, who somehow exert sinister, occult influence on events.

The story is left dangling with the question as to just how and why Theodor became involved in all this. Yet it is not at all "worthless," for it is a milestone in Hoffmann's career. We can see in it certain old and new motifs used in a significant manner. The ideal beloved is now mentally debilitated, but her illness has to do with a mysterious power affecting her lover. (This anticipates Hedwiga in the Kreisler novel in *Kater Murr*.) A nomadic group (cp. *Ignaz Denner*) is associated therewith, as later in *Kater Murr* and *Die Doppeltgänger*. The problem of humdrum existence—"the prosaic"—finds here a new setting, and its solution seems even more difficult than in *Der goldne Topf*.

Finally, the story shows Hoffmann's new awareness of some scarcely surmountable difficulties in penetrating through the empty external phenomena of our world and lives, and into a mythical essence. We are, as one of his characters states, blind moles searching along dark paths, with manifestations of the world above leading us eventually to the light (III, 155 f.). But the way is hard, and Hoffmann's indications as to which path to follow are— like this story—inconclusive. It can be madness to seek anything beyond "the prosaic"—yet he must. This dilemma is at its worst in *Das öde Haus*.

The inconclusiveness of this story is more than compensated for by the following tale, *Das Majorat*, the masterwork of the collection and one of Hoffmann's greatest achievements as a writer. Hoffmann himself recommended it highly in his letter to Kunz (p. 95), and singled it out as the best in a letter to his friend, Hippel (Dec. 15, 1817). It is pervaded with the symbolic atmosphere of the night as none of the others, with the possible exception of *Ignaz Denner*. It is night when Theodor and his great-uncle V. arrive at the old castle. It is night when Theodor, while reading Schiller's *Der Geisterseher*, hears Daniel's ghost for the first time. And it is night when in a remote past, the man-servant, Daniel, murders his master by pushing him through a door into an abyss. As in *Ignaz Denner* and *Die Elixiere des Teufels* this night is all the more sinister for its setting in a German forest, where wolves can suddenly appear and attack people, as when Theodor was hunting. Other sinister figures seem to come alive from the pictures and statues of the dimly-lit castle at night. Thus a typical Hoffmannesque underworld is indicated.

This ghostly background, however, does not comprise a

myth. There are not even any devils inhabiting the night surrounding the locale of R . . . sitten. Only human beings participate in these stories. Even the ghost is motivated by a common personal feeling: that of guilt, and not by universal forces causing him to act according to the laws of some "other world," divorced from immediate concerns.

Even the "other world of music" loses here its former stature. Formerly when a musician sat at a piano singing with a beautiful young lady, he was transported with her into ethereal realms where they experienced a few moments of eternity. Here, when Theodor has such a love affair with the young wife of the baron of the manor at R . . . sitten, his wise and severely candid uncle V. convincingly portrays him as a foolish adolescent, engaging in hopelessly "romantic" nonsense that could have disastrous consequences (III, 192).

In *Das Majorat* there is a previously unknown concern for some of the fundamental problems of everyday life: for family, legal and social matters of the type which were Hoffmann's concern only in his daily work as a lawyer. Associated with this is the obvious warmth and nearness felt toward the main characters, with their human nature perfectly envisioned and portrayed. This is especially true of Theodor's uncle—cantankerous, clever, witty, yet loving and pious—one of Hoffmann's finest character studies. In few works by Hoffmann does an individual human character stand out in such sharp relief and warm vitality.

Also essential problems of human interrelationships are central to the plot, particularly those concerning different generations. In the confrontation of Theodor and V. we see a very young man—inexperienced, "romantically" inclined, and extremely foolish—put in sharp contrast with an elderly and wise old gentleman who can view things with well-informed sobriety. This theme of conflict of generations is then given many variations in the background story, told by V. to Theodor, concerning the history of the family at R . . . sitten, going back to 1760.

The historical aspect implicit here is unusual for Hoffmann, yet it is quite close to the surface, as I attempted to demonstrate in a detailed study of the matter.[1] This amounts to a commentary by Hoffmann on the generation of the last third of the eighteenth century, seen from the quite different circumstances of 1817.

There is no coherent myth embodied in the atmosphere of the *Nachtstücke*. Fragments of myth are present in occasional figures of speech alluding to Satan; in the resemblance of the background to a mythical underworld (the night and the abyss); in certain figures common to other myths, such as that of the master and apprentice; in gold, associated with an evil underworld (the family's treasure store); and in the dark forest of the German fairy tale. But these things do not constitute a myth. Not until the writing of the *Bergwerke zu Falun* did Hoffmann create a coherent nocturnal myth of the underground. The mythical motifs in *Das Majorat* embody an overall symbolism whereby a human situation is deepened through suggestions of a myth. Because of their strongly allegorical nature we may call such themes mythical emblems.

A central figure in this night symbolism is Daniel peering over the edge of an abyss, where formerly stood a tower suggesting the might of a dynasty. Out of these dark depths emerges a story of past crime, horror, hatred, guilt —all of which asserts itself once more in the present, then

[1] "The Allusions to Schiller's *Der Geisterseher* in E. T. A. Hoffmann's *Das Majorat:* Meaning and Background," *German Quarterly,* XXXII (1959), 341-355.

dies forever in ruins. This all happens on earth in dead-earnest actuality, but points beyond itself to fundamental truths like those in a myth. Thus the essence of life is not absent here, as in Hoffmann's usual everyday world, but manifests itself in common experience. In a sense, parts of Hoffmann's personal mythology here take on actuality, and in so doing are no longer myth, but life with a profundity made visible with myth emblems.

The remainder of the *Nachtstücke*, the two stories, *Das Gelübde* and *Das steinerne Herz*, have little relevancy here. *Das Gelübde* is a *Nachtstück* only in the figurative sense of G. H. von Schubert: it deals with psychological aberrations, mixed with a mysterious telepathic power—all part of the "nocturnal side of nature." *Das steinerne Herz* provides a *capriccio* as the final work in Volume Two, like the frame of *Das Sanctus* in Volume One. It also repeats some themes related to the other world of the past, as represented in *Das Majorat*. Otherwise, *Das steinerne Herz* belongs to the *Nachtstücke* for negative reasons: it exorcises the demons of the night with light-hearted persiflage.

The *Nachtstücke* comprise an amorphous collection. The exploration of the demonic nocturnal underworld involved false starts and blind alleys, especially in the second volume. In the first volume, however, *Der Sandmann*, *Ignaz Denner* and *Die Jesuiterkirche in G.* make full use of a symbolic night in which various kinds of demons obtrude into human life. This spell is gradually broken. This is anticipated by the painful buffoonery in the frame of *Das Sanctus*. Then, as was demonstrated, *Das öde Haus* ends in frustrating dilemma and mystification. *Das Majorat*, although one of Hoffmann's greatest accomplishments, takes a totally new direction, out of myth into realistic symbolism and warm-hearted humanity. *Das Gelübde* utilizes a *psychological* "night" symbolism. *Das steinerne Herz* puts the finishing touches to the exorcising of the demons. Thus something new was needed in the materials and techniques of portraying an underworld. Two main trends followed: Hoffmann either explored new areas, or he displaced mythical underworlds into common experience. Thus the *Nachtstücke* contain a tangle of successes and failures in the progress of Hoffmann's career as a writer. Even the failures were not vain efforts, for there is a clear line of development from the *Nachtstücke* into two major works of the time which follows the actual *Nachtstücke* collection (completed in the fall of 1817). These are *Das Fräulein von Scuderi* and *Die Bergwerke zu Falun*, both written the following year.

Das Fräulein von Scuderi appears in the *Serapionsbrüder*, and thus is followed by a critical discussion of the work on the part of the "brothers." The immediate reaction is that the story is truly "Serapiontic," "weil sie, auf geschichtlichen Grund gebaut, doch hinaufsteige ins Phantastische" (VII, 185). Thus the trend of *Das Majorat* is continued here; for it is a story rooted in actual experience, yet has certain fantastic adjuncts. Where *Das Fräulein von Scuderi* "rises into the fantastic," it is a dark night, thus making it a true "Nachtstück." The very first scene, where Olivier attempts to gain entrance to give the jewels to Fräulein von Scuderi, takes place during a night pervaded with fear for the unleashed violence of criminals. Later Olivier under the cover of night tells the whole fearful story of Cardillac's life and heinous crimes. The central figure in this night atmosphere, Cardillac himself, comes out only at night to regain possession of his magnificent works of the jeweler's art by murdering his clients.

The night is simultaneously an appropriate background and the symbolic essence of this greedy and murderous part of his schizophrenic personality. As in *Der Sandmann* and *Ignaz Denner*, there is a connection with Satan, the king of the night, although this complicity is not emphasized and can be regarded as merely metaphorical.[2] It is Hoffmann's night symbolism that reaches here a height of intensity and complexity; the satanic is only suggested.

The foundation for it is laid with masterful artistry in the section following the opening scene. Here Hoffmann only seems to be telling history, describing a crime wave in Paris. What he actually does is proceed from the general to the particular, from the overall picture to the focus, first by telling of the series of poisonings, then of the nocturnal murders by stiletto, supposedly committed by a band of robbers. The particular kind of poison and poisonings in the first case is symbolically significant: it is a "devilish" concoction that can cause death by mere inhalation, leaving no symptoms of poisoning behind. When these poisonings become more and more widespread, there is a sense that the very air is deadly. This intangible aura is made more concrete, but still omnipresent, by the rumors of a large band of murderous thieves circulating through the streets of Paris at night. Here again a fearsome underworld is painted with mysterious, frightening creatures emerging out of the blackness to destroy life and creativity. This mythical emblem is proved, of course, to be unsubstantiated in reality, since Cardillac committed these crimes; but the effect of this image of an underworld remains engraved on the mind as background for the Cardillac story.

2 Cf. VII, 139: 41ff.; also the frequent figures of speech throughout the story using the word "Teufel," "teuflisch," etc.

Thus Cardillac is already characterized before we meet him: his role in the story is to form a focus for the poison and violence of the night. The intensity of this focal symbolism is Hoffmann's consummate artistic achievement in the work. The pitch-black side of Cardillac's character is portrayed with highly pregnant details of great originality. The prenatal influence from his mother, deriving from a sinful obsession with a jewelled necklace and its handsome owner, is a combination of G. H. Schubert's "nocturnal" mumbo-jumbo and Hoffmann's own association of jewels, metals, and other subterranean products with evil and the underworld. Cardillac's art of gold-smithing thus takes on a symbolic superstructure. His obsession with his work leads him into an artist's exclusive scheme of values and behavior in absolute opposition to those of his society, as with Berthold in the *Jesuiterkirche in G.* With this art are also associated other stone and metal objects (of "underworld" origin), such as the "Stein der Weisen" sought by Glaser and Exili in the story, leading to the discovery of the dangerous poison (VII, 134). By the sharp contrast with Cardillac's virtuous "day" identity, his evil nocturnal self is intensified.

The day symbolism of the story, however, is far less rich than that of the night. Yet it is not nearly so colorless as it often is in Hoffmann's tales. The creature standing in opposition to the evil night-wanderer is the magnificent Mlle. de Scuderi herself, standing by her two young protégés, Madelon and Olivier. Olivier is in a somewhat neutral zone as a non-demonic goldsmith (although he is the apprentice of Cardillac), and is the ally of Mlle. de Scuderi. Madelon, however, (as we are repeatedly assured by the author) is a heavenly creature: unfortunately, her earthly being is far less interesting except as a mere role-filler in the story. She does not represent a mythical upper world, such as that in *Der goldne Topf*: this realm is totally absent here. Nor is she convincing as a portrayal of a loving and feminine humanity, as is Klara in *Der Sandmann*.

What opposes the realm of darkness is not the usual mythical world of light and creativity, but rather a fundamental humanity suffering under the violence and delusions brought about by a pestilence of evil in the atmosphere of the time. This all-pervading destructive spirit has managed to penetrate everywhere (even the police is dominated by it: VII, 137: 27), *except into the sanctum of Frl. von Scuderi's conscience*. This moral absolute enabling her to judge others intuitively is severely challenged, causing a Kleistian "Verwirrung des Gefühls" (VII, 157: 40), but she eventually regains her inner composure, along with the accompanying infallible power that opposes the forces of darkness. When appearances are absolutely against Olivier's innocence, her last hope is expressed in the simple words "be human" (VII, 157: 32 and 160: 26).

This is far removed from the resolution of the battle of light and darkness in *Der goldne Topf*. The difference is highly significant and characteristic for Hoffmann's development as an author from 1813 to 1818. Now Hoffmann's concern is far more for the fundamentally human as it manifests itself in living persons, rather than for transcendent forces influencing human life from without, from a primeval and metaphysical distance. We have already observed the beginnings of this shift in emphasis in *Der Sandmann* (Klara) and *Das Majorat* (Grossonkel V ...); even higher manifestations of Hoffmann's humanity appear later in *Kater Murr* (Meister Abraham). This new center for his art is greatly advanced in the character of Frl. von Scuderi, whose prime importance is brought to the fore by the very title of the story, and eventually, by her successful manipulation of events as the instrument of this pivotal point of view.[3]

The power of the story stems from the interaction of absolutes in Cardillac and Fräulein von Scuderi. This confrontation is beautifully—although ironically—expressed by the "betrothal" of Cardillac and Fräulein von Scuderi. A symbolic marriage is suggested toward the beginning of the story when the jewels given her by Cardillac are discussed (VII, 148). The "marriage" is complete when she adorns herself with Cardillac's jewelry. She also wears mourning clothes when she pleads Olivier's case before the king. The deep irony of the situation lies in their diametric opposition to one another, as does the similar juxtaposition of Lindhorst and Liese in *Der goldne Topf*. Here, however, the conflict is not between two myths, but

---

[3] For an interpretation that places positive emphasis on Cardillac rather than Frl. von Scuderi, see Marianne Thalmann's "E. T. A. Hoffmanns 'Fräulein von Scuderi'," *Monatshefte für deutschen Unterricht*, XLI (1949), 107-116. Professor Thalmann's argument is evolved out of Cardillac's majesty as a demonic master-figure and absolutely dedicated artist. Fräulein von Scuderi is seen merely as the "Detektiv auf der Suche nach dem wahren Mörder," and her investigation activity as "ein sehr damenhaftes Abhören von Konfessionen, die ihrer altjüngferlichen Sanftmut zufliegen." I consider this description an unjustified and unnecessary minimization of this grand lady's character. Cardillac's majesty need not be purchased at the expense of the "Fräulein," for they are in totally different categories. There is no reason why we should not allow her gentle, yet powerful humanity and unerring conscience to stand side-by-side with the artist's magnificent demonry in a disturbing, but beautiful dissonance that can be resolved only by Cardillac's "Künstlermärtyrertum." Professor Thalmann portrays Cardillac with a sensitivity and power that is indeed rare among Hoffmann scholars, and I believe her portrayal, in itself, perfectly accurate. But one should not overlook the evergrowing realistic humanism that is present in Frl. von Scuderi and other characters of Hoffmann's later works, culminating in the synthesis of artistic mastery and humanity in Meister Abraham.

between life (intensified by young love), and a symbolic figure and atmosphere originating in an underworld myth. But the myth is on the verge of losing its identity by its incorporation into life.

Die Bergwerke zu Falun is the companion piece of Das Fräulein von Scuderi. These stories—both written toward the end of 1818—comprise a part of the same phase of Hoffmann's writings in that they are more sharply dualistic than at any other point in his life. The two worlds of light and darkness, and their reflections in the double personalities of Cardillac and Elis Fröbom, contrast more severely with each other than such elements in previous works. The areas of conflict are a sympathetically viewed world of actuality (the Olivier-Madelon and Elis-Ulla relationship) and a mysterious dark realm nearby from which destructive figures emerge (the Parisian night inhabited by murderers, and the sinister and dangerous mine of Falun). The symbolic materials of both dark underworlds are the same: stone and metal.

Die Bergwerke zu Falun does not have a pivotal character of such magnificent humanity as Fräulein von Scuderi. In this respect the Bergwerke is obviously a lesser accomplishment. In the Falun atmosphere, however, Hoffmann creates a more extensive and concrete demonic background, which is perhaps a greater accomplishment than the deadly Paris atmosphere. The success of the former stems from the underworld myth that Hoffmann injected into the mine at Falun. Rather than a miasmic night inhabited by murderous thieves, the underworld here has a fully developed and concrete structure. For the first time, Hoffmann is successful in creating a type of "landscape" myth. We have seen indications thereof in Die Jesuiterkirche in G. (see page 78). Also about the same time as when he wrote *Die Bergwerke*, he made a similar attempt at such a myth in *Der unheimliche Gast* (e.g., Angelika's dream: VII, 103f.). These other two works probably could not be successful in this respect because their abode was a conventional Romantic nature landscape, where Hoffmann was not at home. Even the natural phenomena in *Die Bergwerke* were not directly observed. He made a thorough study of books about Falun (in Sweden) and mining, resulting in the use of many terms unknown to the average reader—even of his day—because they were technical or restricted to a knowledge of the Swedish language and geography, thus removing the story somewhat from the common experience of his average readers.

The emergence of the myth of the story is carefully prepared for and motivated. Elis Fröbom, like Anselmus in *Der goldne Topf*, is isolated from society. Elis, however, isolates himself by choice. Besides being a "Neriker"—a member of a melancholy clan of the Swedish nation—he has also lost his parents and two brothers. The most recent bereavement—his mother's death—leaves an empty place in his life that apparently can be filled only by another woman. When Elis has an opportunity to make such an acquaintance near the beginning of the story, however, he rejects it. We are shown the connection between the mother and the girl by the "ostindisches Tuch"—intended for the mother—that he gives the girl upon parting.

With the jubilation of his fellow-sailors and the girls within hearing, he falls into despair, and wishes for death. This utterance evokes the figure of the sinister old miner Torbern out of nowhere. This is the point where the myth breaks through into actuality—although Elis and the reader cannot know that Torbern is from another world until

later. There is, however, a suggestion of a Faustian pact—
making Torbern a Satan-like figure—in the promise to
Elis that, if he becomes a miner, he will be able to see
". . . in dem wunderbaren Gestein die Abspieglung
dessen . . . was oben über den Wolken verborgen" (V,
203). Torbern's world emerges gradually throughout the
sequence of events that follows: Elis' becoming a miner, his
betrothal to Ulla, his growing obsession with the depths,
and his ultimate destruction by the cave-in at the mine.

After Torbern verbally introduces Elis to the fascinating
glitter of underworld metals, Elis has a highly significant
dream. Here typical themes of his old way of life, the sea,
and of his future role as a miner, merge into a weird
landscape in which the water and clouds of a scene at
sea become stone; and beneath the surface of the crystal-
line water magnificent metallic flowers are blossoming
amidst beautiful mermaids. Elis unwittingly commits himself to the underworld forever when he impulsively flings
himself into this "sea," and comes face-to-face with the
queen of this realm; but Elis still can look upward and
see a beautiful creature of the "surface"—who, as is later
learned, is Ulla. Again the connection between the mother
and the other feminine figures is made when his mother's
voice comes from above. The mixture of bliss and horror
in Elis' reaction to all this typifies his subsequent internal
conflict between the influence of the world of the surface
and the lower depths.

Before the lower world appears to him in actuality as a
concrete entity, it takes on the old form already familiar
to us: that of a black, empty abyss. When Elis first sees the
huge open pit of the mine (V, 207), its similarity to other
underworld scenes in Hoffmann is striking: not only does
it have the usual blackness, but also the frightening figures

—for the stones seem to form animal and human images. The typical description of the mine as an "Abgrund" recurs several more times in the story. This time, however, Hoffmann goes far beyond such a vague portrayal, and step-by-step penetrates into an underworld that is concrete and visible.

After Elis becomes a miner, the myth breaks through again with the sudden, inexplicable appearance of Torbern deep in the mine. The purpose of his appearance seems to be to warn Elis that he is being unfaithful to the underworld because of his love for Ulla, and that the "Metallfürst"—a new figure—might take revenge. Thus a masculine figure—a counterpart to Elis' dead father—gives further rounding out of the meaning of the myth for Elis' personal psychology.

As Elis becomes more obsessed with the underworld, he begins to see the metallic plants and beautiful maidens of his dream in the mine itself. He is interrupted by Pehrson Dahlsjö, who has pursued Elis into the mine, and finds him *"wie erstarrt stehend, das Gesicht gedrückt in das kalte Gestein"* (italics mine). Here Elis is beginning to take on the characteristics of the lower depths. Finally, just before his death, the mine seems to promise the revelation of superhuman truths, in fulfillment of Torbern's promise at the beginning that Elis would find a transcendent wisdom in the mine. Elis believes that he will find "den kirschrot funkelnden Almandin" on which his and Ulla's "Lebenstafel" is engraved. This knowledge, far beyond the normal range of human beings, offers the resolution of Elis' conflict, for both temporal and eternal things merge here. There is tragic irony in this, however, for Elis meets his death when he descends into the mine.

Thus the final goal of the underworld and its forces is clearly death. Hoffmann is nowhere else so clear about this. In retrospect, Torbern is discovered to be a kind of angel of death, for he has appeared as a result of Elis' uttering the desire to die. The inexorable sequence leading to the end of the story has an inner necessity growing out of a melancholy man's subconscious but definite desire to escape the bright, sensual world of the surface, thinking he can delve into dark recesses of the mind for greater satisfactions, but failing tragically. The symbolic mine is really a realm of the dead with its beautiful but rigid forms anticipating in a ghastly, hidden symbolism the *rigor mortis* of those who succumb to it. His statuesque form witnessed 50 years later is the final, perhaps somewhat melodramatic touch.

This work is the culmination of Hoffmann's underworld symbolism. Although such realms appear before and after the writing of the *Bergwerke zu Falun*, none takes on such an intense focus and circumscribed locale as the mine at Falun. This is the result of a long development, in which the underworld was constantly scrutinized, remolded and enlarged. It began with the "Reich der Träume" in *Ritter Gluck*; then Hoffmann remolded it into the lower depths of a primeval world in *Der goldne Topf*; then he varied and relocated it in such stories as *Ignaz Denner, Die Jesuiterkirche in G., Der unheimliche Gast* and *Das Fräulein von Scuderi*. Finally, its serious artistic possibilities as a central realm are largely exhausted by *Die Bergwerke zu Falun*.

Now Hoffmann can jest about the underworld as he did with Satan (*Nachricht aus dem Leben eines bekannten Mannes*) after there were no more horrors to write about him. He did just this in the charming fantasy (often neglected by Hoffmann scholars), *Die Königsbraut*, written at the beginning of 1821, about two years after *Die Bergwerke zu Falun*. Hoffmann's imaginary underworld, once portrayed in dead earnest, now gives rise to the purest delight that reading Hoffmann can afford. It is remarkable how the same basic plot and many motifs common to the *Bergwerke zu Falun* could be transformed into such a good-natured parody on the underworld. Here, as with Elis Fröbom, underworld figures emerge into the lives of human beings and attempt to dominate them. In *Die Königsbraut*, however, not only do the "demons" fail, but the characters and action are superbly designed to dispel humorously the spooks of Hoffmann's murky Hades. The central figure, Anna von Zabelthau (rather pretty, but on the plump side) has problems that could be serious. These stem from her bungling recluse father and her fine-frenzied poetic lover. She is, however, a much too simply motivated creature of the earth's surface—a farm girl who wants to get married—to cause us the concern that Elis Fröbom's tortured problems arouse. The father, Dapsul von Zabelthau, is a typical Hoffmannesque "master figure," possessing occult knowledge and powers, but his peccadillos ("Ich fresse erschrecklich!") and frequent bungling at critical moments make him a travesty of such characters as Torbern or Archivarius Lindhorst. The lover, Amandus von Nebelstern, is the self-styled voice of a "higher world," a poet who writes pompous gibberish and inanities that are worth reading only as unconscious self-parody.

Then there is the "underworld" itself. This is *not* primarily the realm of stones and metals—although some of these motifs occur (e.g., VIII, 213:7ff.)—but another realm that was anticipated eight years before in *Der goldne Topf*. It will be remembered that the witch-figure Liese was the offspring of a black dragon feather and a beet root, and that when conquered in the tenth *Vigilie* she was transformed into the latter. Now, in *Die Königsbraut*, Hoffmann expands on this symbolism and creates a whole new sub-kingdom of the underworld, consisting of all varieties of personified bulbous vegetables, ruled over by a gnome, the Vegetable King Daucus Carota I, *alias* Baron Porphyrio von Ockerodastes genannt Corduanspitz. This realm of the underworld, one might suppose, is less deadly than that of Torbern's, simply because it is less subterranean.

Anna von Zabelthau has a slight obsession with these vegetables, which might be compared with Elis' fascination for the mine. This, it seems, makes her more susceptible to the designs of Daucus Carota to marry her than she otherwise might be. Perhaps this is Hoffmann's answer to the question of why Proserpina, goddess of vegetable fertility, should become the queen of Pluto's underworld! In any case, she, like Fröbom, is gradually dominated more and more by subterranean forces until she temporarily acquires their physical characteristics: her head becomes enlarged and she turns yellow, apparently turning into a demi-carrot. (The parallel with Fröbom would be his stone-like rigidity when fetched from the mine by Dahlsjö.) Likewise her father must suffer the indignity of being transformed for a time into a mushroom: he does not quite make the grade to be absorbed into this subcutaneous level of the underworld.

Only once is this good fun interrupted, and then there is some rather frightening grotesquery. This occurs when Dapsul sets aside the spell that causes Daucus Carota and his subjects to appear so affluent and elegant, and, with some whimsical mumbo-jumbo, shows Anna these creatures in their true form: as the epitome of ugliness, wriggling about in a puddle, in "einem farblosen, ekelhaften Schlamm" (VIII, 214 f.). This point of the story approaches the fearsomeness of other areas of Hoffman's underworld, and Anna's reaction contains the same horror

that we have seen in other characters when peering into
an underworld abyss. This horror does not last long,
however, for we are soon led to the grotesque humor of
Anna's feminine vanity when she sees her physical appeal
seriously damaged by her new carrot-like appearance.

The resolution of the story dispels any seriousness that
might possibly remain. This occurs with the conquest of
the demons by the "higher forces" manifested in Amandus
von Nebelstern's "poetry," which causes Daucus Carota
such a terrible stomach-ache that he loses all his power,
then shrinks into his original vegetable form, and Anna's
and her father's normal appearances are restored. Thus a
further parody is added here: that of the "higher world"
of poetry, portrayed seriously (at the end at least) in *Der
goldne Topf*.

The "cosmos" in this story again consists of a high,
middle and lower realm, but the story differs essentially
from *Der goldne Topf*: instead of ending up, like Anselmus, in the upper reaches of eternal beauty, Anna and
Amandus finish their lives together in the amicable, unpoetic world that it was in the first place—a world that
Hoffmann came to love more and more toward the end of
his life.

This did not prevent him from reworking certain materials of his personal mythology, this time drawing heavily
on traditional myths. We have already pointed out the
similarity of this story to the myth of Pluto and Proserpina.
In addition, Hoffmann drew heavily on a favorite book,
Graf von Gabalis oder die verborgenen Wissenschaften,
for the doctrine of the "elemental spirits," which Dapsul
summarizes in the text: "Erfahre . . . dass die tiefe Erde,
die Luft, das Wasser, das Feuer erfüllt ist mit geistigen
Wesen höherer und doch wieder beschränkterer Natur

als die Menschen . . . Gnomen, Salamander, Sylphen und Undinen." (VIII, 191.) Hoffmann had made use of "Elementargeister" before. Archivarius Lindhorst was, "in reality," a salamander. The opera, *Undine*, has a water-sprite as heroine. And, of course, the tale *Der Elementargeist* also has a creature of this category, a salamander. All the traditional mythical sources added together, however, do not constitute Hoffmann's entire mythology, but are merely some of the vocabulary words of his poetic language. Again, as in *Der goldne Topf*, we have pieces of myths drawn from "sources"; but they are incorporated into Hoffmann's personal mythical cosmos: a meaningful, triadically structured universe, with ambiguous blendings of the three realms.

Finally it should be pointed out that in *Die Königsbraut* Hoffmann succeeded to a limited degree in creating another mythical landscape—one that endows nature with a metaphysical depth by using fantastic images. Its subtitle is, after all, "ein nach der Natur entworfenes Märchen." Yet the demonic trend of *Die Bergwerke zu Falun* is still present in it, for the author takes us briefly to the edge of the abyss of the underworld and, for a brief moment, among the fiendish demons themselves. Hoffmann created no fully-formed and consistent myth of a bright, sunny landscape, with one possible and magnificent exception: *Das fremde Kind.*

In *Die Königsbraut*, Hoffmann seems to have exhausted the possibilities of his underworld. After its writing, he did not methodically explore any more areas of it, although its emblems are still utilized as they had been in *Das Fräulein von Scuderi*. Few writers since Dante had explored an underworld so thoroughly as Hoffmann.

7

Märchen: The Child's World of Fantasy

Certain curious features in the chronology of Hoffmann's writings should be observed when generalizing about trends in his literary career. This is particularly true of those directions that led him to extremes, for "les extrêmes se touchent." This applies to Hoffmann as to few other authors.

Amidst Hoffmann's tortured preoccupations around 1817 with demons and their dismal world, he was cultivating a completely different genre—the *Kunstmärchen* which at first were conceived mainly for children. Such stories apparently provided relief from the strains imposed by the demonic tales, as well as solutions to the problems of a man plagued by the dark horrors of a disordered unknown.

The *Kunstmärchen* is not, of course, a completely new trend. *Der goldne Topf* had been written three years before Hoffmann's period of deepest depressions around

1816 and 1817. This *Märchen aus der neuen Zeit* had acted as a counterbalance to Hoffmann's extreme sufferings in Dresden and Leipzig. This would be consistent with Hoffmann's tenet that the function of art is to reveal and create a transcendent world to offset the insufficiencies of the actual one. *Der goldne Topf* would in other contexts be grouped among his other *Märchen*. It was discussed in Chapter II because it belongs to an earlier phase of Hoffmann's career, and also because it is basic to an understanding of all of Hoffmann's subsequent works. Not only does it penetrate far into the fantastic world of Hoffmann's personal mythology, but it also provides the very foundation of this mythical cosmos, shows the relationship of the artist to this and the Philistine world about him, and develops the basic imagery and symbolism of his myths. Although this is true to a degree of Hoffmann's other *Märchen*, none has the all-encompassing, symphonic sweep of *Der goldne Topf*. Yet Hoffmann continued to develop new aspects of this genre, so much so that he completed one major *Märchen* each year from 1816 on: *Nussknacker und Mausekönig* (1816); *Das fremde Kind* (1817); *Klein Zaches* (1818); *Die Brautwahl* (1819); *Prinzessin Brambilla* (1820); *Die Königsbraut* (1821), discussed in the previous chapter; and *Meister Floh* (1822).

The new feature that enters into his *Märchen* from *Nussknacker und Mausekönig* on is a clearly established child's point of view. This is, of course, implicit in *Der goldne Topf*, for Anselmus is child-like in his directness, naïveté, and naturalness. But now actual children enter into the stories, both as audience and participants. No longer having children of his own (his one child, Cäcilie, had died in 1807), Hoffmann often saw Eugenie and Fritz

Hitzig from about 1815 on. They were the daughter and son of Julius Eduard Hitzig, Hoffmann's friend, publisher, and (later) his biographer. Hoffmann's great interest in these children is evidenced by his frequent visits to them, at which he presented them with toys (a home-made castle on one occasion) and told them stories.

This new point of view was, of course, an addition to what came before, but it also imposed limitations, especially if a given story was written expressly as a "child's fairy tale," as were *Nussknacker und Mausekönig* and *Das fremde Kind*. In spite of the deeper implications that Hoffmann could not help but develop in these stories, they had to be appealing on the surface, including much delightful nonsense that should not be taken seriously. Still, an adult cannot read these tales *only* in nostalgic reminiscence of childhood. Hoffmann himself claimed that there were features of them that only a grownup could understand.[1] But there is more than this involved; the child's point of view, observed and formed by sophisticated artistry, is shown to have a wisdom and beauty comparable to that of the primeval world.

Nussknacker und Mausekönig was a long step in the new direction of Hoffmann's *Märchen*. It was a direct outgrowth of Hoffmann's experience with the Hitzig children, and as such is very clearly, and primarily, a *Kindermärchen*, with comparatively few aspects for adults only, yet a completely enjoyable fantasy for any age. It stands in sharp contrast with the heavy gloom of the *Nachtstück* type of tale. This is brought out in the conversations of the *Serapionsbrüder* when the purpose of the *Märchen* is expressly stated as a means of dispelling the gloom of *Die Bergwerke zu Falun* (V, 223).

[1] Cf. V, 271 and VI, 247f.; also *Briefwechsel* I, 256 and II, 2, p. 300.

No better materials for a child's world of fantasy could be chosen than the glittering decorations and toys, and the sweet foods of a German Christmas celebration. No better point of view could be maintained throughout the story than that of Marie Stahlbaum, occasionally supported by that of her younger brother, Fritz. Injected into the story are the attitudes characteristic of these two children: the gentle, protective concern of a little girl, and the aggressiveness of a rambunctious little boy. For the most part, the story is seen through the eyes of Marie. She alone witnesses the battle between the nutcracker's toy army and the mice. Mainly for her benefit, Godfather Drosselmeier tells the story of the hard nut Krakatuk, which is the only cure for the mouse queen's enchantment of Princess Pirlipat. She alone is taken by the Nutcracker— via the sleeve of her father's coat—to the idyllic Never-Never Land of sweets and toys. Finally, her life is most intimately entwined with the fairy-tale world by her eventual "marriage" with Drosselmeier's nephew, who has been transformed into a nutcracker.

The story is delicate and of miniature proportions. The mythical world does not crash through into the life of Marie Stahlbaum, as it does when Anselmus upsets Liese's applecart: on the contrary, it is introduced by gentle rustling and music. More important, there is no jolting reorientation in the transition, for here familiar toys simply come to life. Even the "nocturnal" aspects of the story— such as a demonic world of mice emerging during the witching hour—is made less sinister by the diminutive size of the assailants, and the identity of the assailed as toys. Furthermore, the background myth about Princess Pirlipat and the Nutcracker is full of good humor and whimsy: a king who sets his queen to work making sausage; a baby princess born with a full set of teeth; the mirthful mumbo-jumbo of the kratatuk cure; a fairy-tale land at the end of Papa's coat sleeve. Besides, this is a fairy tale, and we therefore know from the start that all will turn out well in the end.

Thus the story is mainly for delight, not for instruction. What, then, does it contain that is exclusively for grown-ups? Surely there are more than a few details thrown in to inflate the self-esteem of more sophisticated minds, such as the quotation from Shakespeare, and the obvious reference to an omnipotent God (the "Confectioner") in the fairy-tale candyland (V, 238 and 265, resp.).

The plot is certainly more complex than the average child of eight or ten can follow comfortably. But the most "grown-up" aspect of it emerges from a comparison with the less childlike *Der goldne Topf*. Here we have the same basic image groups and motifs: a glittering, idyllic upper realm of myth; an underworld of sinister creatures; a problematical figure (Marie) standing between them, as well as between the whole mythical realm and the actual world. These are the things that would keep us from labelling the story "childish." At the same time we can enjoy its childlike qualities and point of view. Thus again Hoffmann evoked his universal world of poetic images, and put them into action with one another—not so much to teach us anything, but to delight us with their fantastic forms and interactions.

Nussknacker und Mausekönig is not a well-integrated story. Its myriad of motifs cannot be traced to a concentrated background myth as in *Der goldne Topf*; the story of Princess Pirlipat was not conceived to be the story of the Creation and its direct outgrowths. One major feature of the story—Pate Drosselmeier's role—contains some con-

tradiction. There is no justification for his refusal to help
Marie conquer the mice in the beginning of the story, nor
for his strangely crotchety attitude toward Marie's whole
fantastic world—culminating in the apparent falsehood of
his statement that he had given Marie the Mouse King's
crowns years before, and used to wear them on his watch-
chain. This occurs after he has warmly praised her imaginary world (V, 254). His proper role should be, it
seems, that of a Lindhorst, a "Geisterfürst." What strange
whimsy prompted Hoffmann to make him so contradictory
is difficult to say. Perhaps he felt a need to create a character along the lines of the grotesque and fearful Magister
Tinte in *Das fremde Kind.* Or perhaps this is all excessive
"adult" bickering and fussing. In any case, the primary
purpose of the story—to delight children—is still served in
the form in which we have it.

Hoffmann's next fairy tale, *Das fremde Kind* (1817),
represents a conscious effort to develop his skill further in
this genre, rectifying certain features that he had considered errors in *Nussknacker und Mausekönig.* In the
conversations of the *Serapionsbrüder* he severely criticized
his delightful nutcracker story through Lothar, the narrator, who claims "[dass] ein gewisser unverzeihlicher
Übermut darin herrscht und ich zu sehr an die erwach-
senen Leute und ihre Taten gedacht . . . und ich gelobe
euch, weniger in phantastischem Übermut zu luxurieren,
frömmer, kindlicher zu sein" (V, 273). The phrasing of
the last part of this quotation, "frömmer, kindlicher zu
sein," is repeated in the introductory passage of *Das
fremde Kind.*

Yet Hoffmann still claimed that *Das fremde Kind* has
its adult aspects that a child would not understand. In
comparing it with *Nussknacker und Mausekönig* he

claims: "es ist reiner, kindlicher und eben deshalb für Kinder, *fassen sie auch nicht die tiefere Idee des Ganzen,* brauchbarer." (Italics mine; letter to Kunz, March 8, 1818.) He becomes ironical about this aspect of the story in the discussion after it is told to the *Serapionsbrüder*: "einige verdammte Schnörkel, deren tieferen Sinn das Kind nicht zu ahnen vermag, hast du doch nicht weglassen können." Furthermore, he places the story into the category of "Märchen für kleine und grosse Kinder" (VI, 247). The attitude behind these statements is, perhaps, exaggerated. They illustrate, however, some genuinely serious intent on Hoffmann's part.

The overall plot of *Das fremde Kind* closely resembles that of its predecessor. Two children, a girl and a boy, are visited by the agents of a new world of fantasy, entering abruptly into their lives. The nature of this world is then revealed in a central myth, which reflects the underlying powers of the everyday world. There is a conflict of higher and lower forces, it is resolved, they live happily ever after.

These superficial similarities, however, can be misleading. In *Das fremde Kind*, the scene is shifted from Christmas, with its toys and candy, and from their donor (Drosselmeier), to that of the romantic nature landscape of a German forest. Here the figures and motifs of the toys in *Nussknacker und Mausekönig* assume a malevolent connotation, for they are associated with conventional false and cruel methods of rearing and educating children. Although Drosselmeier was sympathetically portrayed as one who unveils a poetic realm to children, he nevertheless had a strongly ambiguous role and appearance. Now this sinister side of the master figure is recast into an unambiguous, tormenting demon: Pepser, the Gnome-King, alias Pepasilio, alias Magister Tinte.

Pepser's opponent is the Child-Stranger, the central figure of Hoffmann's most highly developed nature myth. Although originally from a fairy-tale land, the Child-Stranger's earthly realm is the forested landscape that is the subject of so many German Romantic paintings. Like Parzival, this child speaks the language of birds and plants. Like almost all mythical figures in Hoffmann, he comes onto the scene abruptly at a low point in the lives of the persons concerned, in this case, the young children Felix and Gottlieb, who have thrown away the toys given them by their stuffy, pedantic relatives and are yearning for more satisfying activity. The Child-Stranger is characteristically introduced by music. His physical features are the ideal of beauty of all imaginary worlds: "lilienweisses Gesicht, rosenrote Wangen, kirschrote Lippen, blauglänzende Augen und goldgelocktes Haar . . ." (VI, 226). Highly unusual, however, is that he appears in different forms to different sexes: in Felix's eyes he is a boy, and in Gottlieb's a girl. This ingeniously reflects his true nature as a creature from a world incommensurable with actuality. A passage from Milton aptly describes such beings:

> For Spirits when they please
> Can either Sex assume, or both; so soft
> And uncompounded is their Essence pure,
> Not ti'd or manacl'd with joynt or limb,
> Nor founded on the brittle strength of bones,
> Like cumbrous flesh; but in what shape they choose
> Dilated or condens't, bright or obscure,
> Can execute thir aerie purposes,
> And works of love or enmity fulfill.
> (*Paradise Lost* I)

Thus the Child-Stranger and his world are not viewed from a single, simple point of view, as that of Marie in *Nussknacker und Mausekönig*, but they suggest a kaleidoscopic symbolism, that shifts in meaning from one viewer to the next. The childlike point of view does, of course, impose a limitation. This limitation is not very restrictive, however, especially at the end of the story, for here the most adult person of all the characters—the father—also enters into the children's preoccupation with the other world as he reminisces over the hitherto forgotten time when he saw the Child-Stranger in his own childhood.

This is one of Hoffmann's most "open" symbolic figures. The child and his world are represented with great concreteness, but this is combined with an indeterminate number of perspectives from which we may view him. Even the most obvious interpretation—the Child-Stranger as the Christ-Child—is left open, for he is never called that, nor are there any definite restrictive aspects to the story making a Christian interpretation compelling. In a few details one might find evidence for this, such as at the end when satanic figures of the Christian variety are possibly alluded to in the Child-Stranger's final words to Felix and Gottlieb: "Behaltet mich nur treu im Herzen, wie ihr es bis jetzt getan, dann vermag der böse Pepser und *kein anderer Widersacher* etwas über euch." (VI, 246; italics mine.) The Christian interpretation is, however, only suggested. The reader may carry this line of thought further, as he chooses, just as the children can see him either as a boy or a girl.[2]

In any case, the child is a being from a transcendent realm that closely resembles those in other tales: it is an ideal state, sensually represented by a light and airy atmosphere, filled with the color and aroma of flowers, and re-

[2] Also in *Die Elixiere des Teufels* there is a similarly elusive "child stranger." This one, however, definitely suggests Jesus as a child, for one of the games that he plays with Medardus consists of laying out stones in the form of a cross (II, 24).

sounding with the perfect harmony of a sublime music. This other world, however, is less accessible than those in the other tales. When Felix and Gottlieb express the wish to go to the Child-Stranger's native land, he sadly informs them that this is not in the order of things. This contrasts with Marie's journey to the "other world," which she visits at the unsolicited invitation of the nutcracker. The same applies to Anselmus' presence in Atlantis. In *Das fremde Kind*, however, this world is removed to a region that is scarcely imaginable, and is not visited by the human beings in the story. It can be described, as the Child-Stranger does, but only some of its powers and agents manifest themselves in the lives of human beings; its total reality remains transcendent.

The source of the motifs of this imaginary world is nature. Not only, however, is myth revealed in nature scenes to children, the most natural of human creatures; also in the kingdom off in the clouds, the ministers of the court are elemental spirits of air, water, and fire (VI, 232 f.)—with the earth spirit playing the role of opposition. (The latter's absence suggests the unearthly, "aethereal" nature of this realm.) When this world breaks into actuality, it destroys all previously known orders and supplants its equivalents for things of common experience. Thus children's toys—the hunter, the harpman, and the doll—are shown to be empty and ugly, and are replaced by a castle, and other dolls and toy huntsmen made directly out of live plants. In like manner, Pepser's efforts to "educate" Felix and Gottlieb are eventually replaced by the contemplation of nature embodied in the image of the Child.

The outcome of the story is unusual for Hoffmann, and for any children's fairy tale. The death of the children's father, and the complete destitution of the family are scarcely common materials for children's entertainment. Yet this ending is strangely appropriate to illustrate conclusively the Child-Stranger's power to console and revive human beings overcome by grief, especially when he appears to the family on the road to their new home. Or, in broader terms, it is shown how "the other world"—in this case partly within us and partly inherent in nature—is a constantly accessible refuge, as well as a source of new life.

In this story, Hoffmann's other world is a curious combination of remoteness and nearness. The remoteness keeps it superior to common experience; yet it is close by, because its agents in nature make it accessible. The child's ingenuous point of view, and a cosmic image of the sources of life and form—such elusive opposites of nearness and inaccessibility—make *Das fremde Kind* a high point in Hoffmann's literary production.

It seems inconceivable that Hoffmann could develop the child's point of view to a greater sublimity and purity than he did in *Das fremde Kind*. If, then, he were to continue his dynamic progress in the genre, a totally new path would seem inevitable. This, in any case, was what happened when Hoffmann wrote his *Märchen* for the following year, 1818.

Klein Zaches was apparently conceived under the shadow of an illness that brought its author near death, as is made so poignantly clear by Hoffmann's letter to Holbein of June 13, 1818. Symptoms of this are the many deeply personal aspects of the story, involving feelings of guilt and inadequacy—things one is likely to ponder in the face of death. Hoffmann's own unattractive appearance and behavior, bordering on the grotesque,[3] are surreal-

---

[3] See J. E. Hitzig's description of him in *Aus Hoffmann's Leben und Nachlass* (Berlin, 1823), II, 297ff.

istically re-formed into the inhumanly ugly "Wechselbalg," Klein Zaches genannt Zinnober. Thus the emphasis shifts from childlike lightness and playfulness to a bizarre humor that sometimes borders on hysteria, and suggests dark undertones of tragic seriousness.

Hoffmann took more than usual personal interest in *Klein Zaches* and its impression on his readers, partly because he considered it a good work, but also apparently because of its fascination for him as a revelation of himself. That it was intended to be humorous (or that Hoffmann hoped it would be considered as such) is evidenced in the first few mentionings of it in his correspondence. In the first letter he called the story "die Geburt einer etwas ausgelassenen ironisierenden Fantasie," and its hero "den humoristischen Wechselbalg" (to Pückler, 24 Jan. 1819). Three days later when he wrote to his friend Hippel, he referred to it as "das tolle Märchen," and claimed that it was "das humoristischste, was ich geschrieben, und von meinen hiesigen Freunden als solches anerkannt." A little over a week later, he called it "mein sicher wahnsinniges Buch" (to Kralowsky, Feb. 5, 1819). Hoffmann seems to have been protesting its humor a little too much, and the particular brand of humor here is surely not very light-hearted or good-natured. It is the kind that grows out of grief. Thus we can challenge Hoffmann's own comment on *Klein Zaches* in the introduction to *Prinzessin Brambilla*: "Das Märchen 'Klein Zaches, genannt Zinnober' . . . enthält nichts weiter als die lose lockre Ausführung einer scherzhaften Idee. Nicht wenig erstaunte indessen der Autor, als er auf eine Rezension stiess, in der dieser zu augenblicklicher Belustigung ohne allen weitern Anspruch leicht hingeworfene Scherz mit ernsthafter wichtiger Miene zergliedert und sorgfältig jeder Quelle erwähnt wurde, aus der der Autor geschöpft haben sollte.

. . ." It is not "ein Buch für Leute, die alles gern ernst und wichtig nehmen" (X, 21). Again, Hoffmann appears to be protesting too much. Also, it does not necessarily follow that *Zaches* is not a serious work just because he did not use the sources in question. Arguments against this view should not be overstated either. The contention here is merely that Hoffmann could not always clearly perceive the true nature and merit of his literary works when they revealed deeply personal problems, and that here, in spite of the genuine humor of the work, he instinctively repressed, ignored, or denied a fearsome side that necessarily is implicit in any grotesquery.[4]

The originality of the central figure *Klein Zaches* is striking. From birth onward, Zaches' appearance scarcely allows him a place in the animal kingdom, to say nothing of the human realm:

Das was man auf den ersten Blick sehr gut für ein seltsam verknorpeltes Stückchen Holz hätte ansehen können, war nämlich ein kaum zwei Spannen hoher, missgestalteter Junge, der von dem Korbe, wo er querüber gelegen, heruntergekrochen, sich jetzt knurrend im Grase wälzte. Der Kopf stak dem Dinge tief zwischen den Schultern, die Stelle des Rückens vertrat ein kürbisähnlicher Auswuchs, und gleich unter der Brust hingen die haselgertdünnen Beinchen herab, so dass der Junge aussah wie ein gespalteter Rettich. Vom Gesicht konnte ein stumpfes Auge nicht viel entdecken, schärfer hinblickend, wurde man aber wohl die lange spitze Nase, die aus schwarzen struppigen Haaren hervorstarrte, und ein paar

---

[4] Cf. the definition by Lee B. Jennings, "Gottfried Keller and the Grotesque," *Monatshefte*, L (1958): "the fearsome made ludicrous in freakish form" (p. 9). See also W. Kayser, *Das Groteske* (Oldenburg und Hamburg, 1957): "das Groteske ist die entfremdete Welt . . . Es geht beim Grotesken nicht um Todesfurcht, sondern um Lebensangst." (198 f.)

kleine, schwarz funkelnde Äuglein gewahr, die, zumal bei den übrigens ganz alten, eingefurchten Zügen des Gesichts, ein klein Alräunchen kundzutun schienen. (IV, 110.)

The predominance of vegetable organisms in the similes (Holz, Kürbis, Haselgert, Rettich, Alräunchen) make up the grotesquery of the description. This is all brought into a severe clash with the new features that Zaches' "fairy godmother," Rosabelverde, bestows on him with her magic spell, whereby "alles, was in seiner Gegenwart irgendein anderer Vortreffliches denkt, spricht oder tut, auf *seine* Rechnung kommen . . . muss" (IV, 170: 7-12). Rosabelverde's purpose is not to unleash a mirthful havoc on society (as she subsequently does), but to give Klein Zaches *external* gifts that are to radiate and penetrate into his innermost being and, ultimately, actually convert him into that which he originally only seemed to be (IV, 186: 26 ff.). The failure of Rosabelverde's designs produces Zaches' ultimate tragedy.

There is nothing to match Zaches' grotesqueness in Hoffmann's other writings, with the possible exception of *Rat Krespel*. He appears, however, amidst a setting and characters that are not at all unique in Hoffmann. In fact, much of the story consists of elements of *Der goldne Topf*. The real "hero" of the story, Balthasar, is like Anselmus— a dreamy young man at odds with society. He is chosen by Prosper Alpanus, a representative of the mythical world, to become a poet. This ultimately entails appropriation of a kind of Atlantis—here Prosper Alpanus' estate, bequeathed to Balthasar at the end of the story. Parallel to Serpentina is Candida, who shares Balthasar's new estate when all the vicissitudes of the story are past. These striking similarities with *Der goldne Topf* and their successful remolding and execution might lead one to judge it by exactly the same criteria. This should not be done, for there are some important differences.

First and foremost: the main enemy of poetry in this case is *not* the underworld, represented by a witch or satanic figures. Balthasar and Prosper Alpanus are thwarted by Klein Zaches and the society which erroneously believes him to be handsome and wise. Klein Zaches is not an evil and destructive agent of the underworld, nor is there an underworld influence clearly indicated anywhere in the story. To make sure that such influence is ruled out, Hoffmann has Prosper Alpanus show Balthasar a kind of rogues' gallery of "Wurzelmänner" and earth spirits in an attempt to establish the exact "spiritual" identity of the culprit Klein Zaches. After Balthasar has gone through all the illustrations of these spirits without finding Klein Zaches, Prosper Alpanus comes to the clear-cut conclusion: "Es ist . . . nunmehr gewiss, dass der missgestaltete Zinnober weder ein Wurzelmann noch ein Erdgeist ist, sondern ein gewöhnlicher Mensch." (IV, 154.) Never before has the so-called "Gespenster-Hoffmann" allowed so much disorder to be wrought on society by "an ordinary human being." This is the unusual feature about *Klein Zaches*.

It is overstating the case, however, to call Klein Zaches an "ordinary human being" without qualification. What Hoffmann apparently means to emphasize here is that Zaches is *not* of the spirit world. As a human being, he certainly leaves much to be desired by way of human features. It is this very lack of humanness that makes it necessary to pronounce Zaches human on the basis of Prosper Alpanus' indisputable authority. This pronouncement is called for because Hoffmann has bestowed upon him all the externalities of one of his subterranean vegetable spirits. In addition to the passage above, describing Klein Zaches, he is repeatedly likened to various vegetables throughout the book, as well as to a cat and a monkey, which are favorite pets of witches, appearing, for example, in Liese's abode in *Der goldne Topf*. Zaches' mother, Liese, also bears her name. And let it not be forgotten that one of Liese's parents was a "Runkelrübe"! Hoffmann could not have attached many more emblems to Zaches to indicate that his origin is in the underworld—yet he takes pains to disprove this origin, and thus to remove his usual enemy of poetry, in order to create a different one.

The counterforce to Prosper Alpanus' influence is provided by Rosabelverde, who exists apparently on the same level of the primeval world as he. Early in the story it is emphasized that she is *not* a witch, by ascribing her alleged witchcraft to rumor (IV, 115). She is *not* his traditional enemy as was Liese of Lindhorst, nor did she originally intend to oppose his designs. She simply tried to convert a lower order of human being to a higher one, as Prosper was doing with Balthasar, by the process already described, and produced thereby unforeseen and undesired results. In other words, it was all a mistake! And she admits this to Prosper Alpanus in their last discussion with each other, whereupon they part as friends.

If there is any real counterforce to poetry in the story it is a stuffy, rationalistic society. As part of the "installation of the Enlightenment," the representatives of the poetic world—magicians, fairies, and the like—are expressly forbidden to maintain residence in Paphnutius' kingdom —Prosper Alpanus and Rosabelverde being the only exceptions. It is this society which is the real force behind Klein Zaches, once the spell is cast, and is in unwitting complicity with him to take away the merits of others by making them appear to belong to him. And these other persons—poets, musicians, handsome persons, wise men— are portrayed as being sympathetic with Balthasar and hence with the whole kingdom of poetry.

The conflict, then, is between an anti-mythical Philistine society, such as that presented in *Der goldne Topf* (Heerbrand and Paulmann), and the world of poetry. In general, this particular conflict is more clearly and concretely represented than in *Der goldne Topf*, in which the Philistine world was at times more or less neutral, and at other times only unconsciously furthering the aims of Liese and the underworld. In *Klein Zaches*, there is no real underworld to detract from society's role as the opponent. In a sense, society here becomes an underworld, or something resembling it, by having its attention centered on a creature emblematic of such a realm—who is, however, as Hoffmann insists, an "ordinary human being." In any case, society here represents a world lower than that of Prosper Alpanus, if not really an "underworld" in our previous definition of the term.

The conflict between society and art is also pointed up by the obvious parallelism of Prosper Alpanus, the genuine "Magus," and Mosch Terpin, the superficial "scientist" whose science consists of such activities as proving that darkness is the absence of light. Thus the Alpanus-Terpin conflict corresponds to that of Lindhorst and Liese. This applies even to the poet's beloved in question: the enemy of poetry tries to prevent a marriage with a poet.

In general, society is depicted here far more extensively and more as a genuine force in the tale than in *Der goldne Topf*. The realm of poetry, on the other hand, is not presented so fully and coherently. There is no central myth to which all can be traced: instead we have several fragments of one, involving Prosper Alpanus and his origins in the primeval world of Ancient India, Egypt, and "Dschinnistan," and another myth connected with Rosabelverde (IV, 164 and 169). This amounts to little, compared with the myths in the third and eighth *Vigilien* of *Der goldne Topf*.

This is all consistent with the trend toward the end of Hoffmann's life when he frequently de-emphasizes transcendent myths and lets everyday life and humanity take on a reality and poetry hitherto unknown in his earlier, more fantastic works. We have seen this kind of realism in *Das Majorat* and *Das Fräulein von Scuderi*. But we have also seen, as in *Klein Zaches*, that many elements of his mythical world were preserved and employed in the form of symbolism. In *Klein Zaches* a kind of humanism is proposed, albeit in a negative way. Zaches, Hoffmann insists, is a human being. This being the case, we would have to formulate the problem of the story as that of an absolutely "unpoetic" (ugly and stupid) person who is constitutionally unable to become "poetic," no matter how many emblems of poetry are bestowed upon him. This situation has its humor, it is true. *Klein Zaches* even dies a "humorous death" (IV, 187: 35). Such a death, however, cannot fail to have something of the grotesque in it, which in turn is accompanied by a highly serious note. Klein Zaches' demise is thus also called, by Hoffmann himself, "a tragic death" (IV, 191: 4); and his appearance and people's attitude toward him in death have a beauty and dignity that make the story far more than the joke that Hoffmann claims it to be two years later in the introduction to *Prinzessin Brambilla*.

The first phase in the development of Hoffmann's late

Märchen, as traced in this chapter, took a strange course indeed: from the most idyllic childlike atmosphere of *Nussknacker und Mausekönig* and *Das fremde Kind*, to the dissonant grotesqueness in *Klein Zaches*. The latter's sinister aspects were prepared for in the children's stories, however, by the demonic features in Drosselmeier and Magister Tinte. Also, *Klein Zaches* represents in part a retrogression back to the mood of the *Nachtstücke*. There now came a highly mature phase in which a balance and blending of the extremes present in the above stories ensued, and the cosmic harmony of *Der goldne Topf* was restored, although less so on the purely mythical level, and more in human society. At the same time, new areas of concern were explored, and new narrative techniques utilized.

8

Märchen: Further Developments of the Cosmic Myth

Between the two major *Märchen, Klein Zaches* and *Prinzessin Brambilla* came *Die Brautwahl,* written in 1819, then revised for the *Serapionsbrüder* in 1820. This revision was undertaken to remove some materials that were meaningful only to a Berlin audience, for whom the story was originally written. The attention that this work has received has been due mainly to the local patriotism of Hans von Müller, who prepared a definitive, annotated edition of the original version in 1910. As for artistic merit, this tale is hardly worth such attention, for this is one of the several potboilers that Hoffmann wrote toward the end of his life, sandwiched amidst some of his finest works. Hans von Müller himself defined Hoffmann's role at this time as "Dichter und schlechter Unterhaltungs- schriftsteller."[1] Although the beginning of the story showed some promise of being "dichterisch," in its final

[1] *Briefwechsel* II, 2, p. 309.

form it turned out to be little more than light entertainment, containing almost nothing that is essentially new in the exploration of Hoffmann's poetic world.

There are two typical Hoffmannesque "background stories" in the tale: one relates to Manasse, a Jew; the other to the goldsmith, Leonhard. Manasse is, "in reality," the "Münzjude" Lippold who was once executed for practicing black magic, and now wanders about, a second Ahasverus, the traditional "wandering Jew." Leonhard also is strongly suspected of being a revenant, and was known in his former life as Leonhard Turnhäuser. Hoffmann exploited here the main features of Francesco I in *Die Elixiere des Teufels* for a bit of spooky diversion. The wandering Jew identity, the revenant figure, the artist type (suggested by "Leonhard," or "Leonardo," the name Hoffmann reserves for artists)—such motifs as these seem derived from *Die Elixiere des Teufels*. A hint of demonry is then added to Leonhard by making him a goldsmith (as with Cardillac in *Das Fräulein von Scuderi*). Edmund and Albertine correspond to Olivier and Madelon. An amusing *Spiessbürger*, Tusmann, completes the picture. Thus a now threadbare plot is set up and run off once more with little real variation.

Two details of the story are relevant here. One is the Jewish "Dales" legend, having little bearing on the story, but interesting in itself (VII, 63 f.). Dales is an allegorical figure standing for poverty, a creature who enters a household and becomes ever larger and more robust-looking as the family's poverty increases. This intriguing figure was not, unfortunately, used or varied in any other work by Hoffmann. The other matter is contained in the conversation between Leonhard and Edmund concerning a painting, "eine schöne Baumgruppe nach der Natur" on which

Edmund is working. Here Leonhard says: ". . . ich meine, aus den dicken Blättern da guckten allerlei Gestalten heraus im buntesten Wechsel, bald Genien, bald seltsame Tiere, bald Jungfrauen, bald Blumen. Und doch sollte das Ganze wohl nur sich zu jener Baumgruppe uns gegenüber gestalten durch die die Strahlen der Abendsonne so lieblich funkeln." (VII, 36.) This is one of Hoffmann's better verbal paintings of a landscape mythology, which was discussed as a pictorial matter in the *Jesuiterkirche in G.*, then put into a literary form in *Das fremde Kind* and *Die Königsbraut*. Here, however, it remains unfulfilled, like the rest of the story.

Hoffmann's *Märchen* for the year 1820, *Prinzessin Brambilla*, is his most controversial work. Interpretations of it vary from grudgingly lukewarm to ardently enthusiastic. Opinions have been spread over this range since its publication in 1821.[2] It is not the purpose here to settle this controversy, but to discuss the "other world" in *Prinzessin Brambilla*, and thereby, it is hoped, to avoid serious misconceptions that can arise due to its complexity, and provide at least a few solid points of departure in this most elusive of Hoffmann's tales.

The milieu is Rome during the carnival season; the happenings are mainly connected with the love of Giglio

---

2 For a summary of various first reactions, see Georg Ellinger's Introduction, *Werke*, X, 8 ff., and also Harich, II, 319 f. Heinrich Heine claimed, "Wer über der Prinzessin Brambilla nicht den Kopf verliert, hat keinen zu verlieren." Baudelaire said that it offered a whole school of aesthetics. Harich himself refers to it flatly as "Von allen Dichtungen Hoffmanns seine gelungenste." Von Müller seems to favor those who disapproved, although he mentions those proposing the opposite view (*Briefwechsel* II, 2, p. 417 f.). Von Schaukal, on the other hand, has strongly mixed feelings about it (p. 202 ff.). Von Schenck praises it (p. 399 ff.). Hewett-Thayer calls it "one of the most baffling, most subtly intriguing, products of the creative imagination" (p. 233) and "a brilliant, effervescent product of Hoffmann's imagination" (p. 235).

and Giacinta as they come to know each other ever more intimately during a stormy courtship, and finally marry. Giglio is an actor and Giacinta becomes an actress at the end of the book after giving up her work as a seamstress. Machinating much of the plot is the charlatan Celionati, alias the Duke of Pistoja, who is attempting to reform the Roman theater, ridding it of wooden tragedies full of melodrama and pathos, and substituting lively, imaginative comedies. Giglio provides the focal point in the course of this transition, for he is one of the most popular tragic actors, whom Celionati would oppose. Celionati succeeds in his attempt, Giglio and Giacinta become comic actors, and find happiness together. The means of achieving this is a bewildering plot involving fictitious mask identities of Giacinta (as Princess Brambilla) and Giglio (as Prince Chiapperi).

It is difficult to see through the tangled web of events into these happenings on first reading. The story progresses in dream-like sequences, with much mystification and delightful confusion. Hoffmann adds to the difficulties in interpreting the work by warning us in the foreword: "Um nun jedem Missverständnis vorzubeugen, erklärt der Herausgeber dieser Blätter im voraus, dass ebensowenig, wie 'Klein Zaches,' die 'Prinzessin Brambilla' ein Buch ist für Leute, die alles gern ernst und wichtig nehmen." (X, 21.) He reinforces this by calling the tale a "Capriccio" in the subtitle and repeatedly throughout the text—once even "ein durchaus erlogenes Capriccio!" (X, 100.) The extemporaneity of the work is further suggested by the series of carnival etchings by Jacques Callot, ostensibly chosen at random and providing the sequence and point of departure for most of the scenes.

This need not inhibit us from looking for the most

serious and subtle artistry in the work. In fact, Hoffmann's very over-insistence upon its being an artless capriccio evokes suspicion, an awareness that Hoffmann is joking about his jokes, and being highly artful in his artlessness. This comes to light upon considering that Hoffmann did not use all the etchings in the Callot series, and he re-arranged those that he did use, employing considerable inventive interpretation for the purposes of his story. On the whole, then, we must regard Hoffmann's downgrading of his art as part of the Romantic irony of the work, and we can approach the work seriously without qualms, just as we can be serious about the most ironic of romantically ironic books, *Don Quixote*. This comparison is no accident. There is apparently considerable influence of Cervantes' *Don Quixote* in *Prinzessin Brambilla*. Evidence for this is: the allusion to Sancho Panza in the text of the work (X, 67); the multiple interplays and mirrorings of fiction and reality, especially as in Part II of *Don Quixote*, which abounds with fiction created by characters to correspond to Don Quixote's imaginary world; Hoffmann's alleged role as merely the "editor" of the story; and Hoffmann's great interest in Cervantes, dating back to the Bamberg period and *Berganza*, a sequel to a Cervantes novella.

Like *Der goldne Topf, Prinzessin Brambilla* has an elaborate and complete central myth set in primeval times. This is the story of the "Urdarquelle," narrated in Chapter III, continued in Chapter V, then supplemented from time to time, especially at the ends of Chapters VI and VIII. Unlike the myth of *Der goldne Topf*, its beginning is somewhat later than the Creation, for it is immediately after the *Urzeit*. This myth does not have such a fundamental, cosmic quality and structure as does that in *Der goldne Topf.* There is, however, a more coherent story in it. It is centered on the "Urdarquelle," which with the aid of Hermod, a magician, changes King Ophioch's chronic sadness into mirth when the king sees his own reflection mirrored on its surface. This event is part of the eternal cycle of the Phoenix-like rebirth of human spiritual forces that have been dead or dormant. When King Ophioch and Queen Liris die, the cycle is repeated as the kingdom first mourns, then rejoices at the appearance of Princess Mystilis in the calyx of a lotus flower. This repetition of the cycle is halted, however, by the demon Typhon, who transforms Mystilis into a miniature china doll, and causes the kingdom to revert to sadness, and the "Urdarquelle" to dry up. In order that Mystilis and her subjects might peer into a clear, full "Urdarquelle" again, "the variegated bird" must be caught with netting woven by delicate hands (a favorite activity both of Liris and Mystilis). This sequence is completed in the "real" sections of the book when, at the palace, Giglio is captured after turning into "der bunte Vogel." Thus the spell is broken and Mystilis (the "real" identity of both Princess Brambilla and Giacinta), her subjects, and the transformed Giglio can then see themselves and each other in the "Urdarquelle."

This myth and its extension into actuality embodies the idea to which Hoffmann refers in the foreword. The "idea" concerns the process of loss of "Anschauung"—a perception and experiencing of the total unity of the world—through empty, often abstract thought. It is summed up in slight variations of a formula beginning, "Der Gedanke zerstörte die Anschauung." With reference to King Ophioch's first depression, this phrase is followed by: ". . . aber dem Prisma des Kristalls, zu dem die feurige

Flut im Vermählungskampf mit dem feindlichen Gift gerann, entstrahlt die Anschauung neugeboren, selbst Fötus des Gedankens!" (X, 61.) This cryptic formula describes a process of rebirth, arising out of a combination of higher and lower forces ("feurige Flut" and "feindliches Gift," respectively), as in the myth of *Der goldne Topf*. Then the basic formula is put into more specifically human terms: "Der Gedanke zerstört die Anschauung, und losgerissen von der Mutter Brust wankt in irrem Wahn, in blinder Betäubtheit der Mensch heimatlos umher, bis des Gedankens eignes Spiegelbild dem Gedanken selbst die Erkenntnis schafft, dass er *ist*, und dass er in dem tiefsten, reichsten Schacht, den ihm die mütterliche Königin geöffnet, als Herrscher gebietet, muss er auch als Vasall gehorchen." (X, 64 f.) Man, when he is without "Anschauung," wanders in solitude, without any integration into the world. He achieves reintegration by a process of self-perception, of seeing himself in the depths of a "mirror"—here the "Urdarquelle"—bestowed on him by divine powers.[3] In this sequence, lack of self-awareness is practically equated with sadness, and regaining it with joy. Thus the immediate reaction to seeing oneself is laughter, which is defined here as the expression of "Freude über den Sieg innerer geistiger Kraft" (X, 64). Thus, in the last analysis, the story describes a certain line of development taken by individual human beings; and all the fantastic, puzzling hocus-pocus of the tale is resolved in the release of innate personality, or, more simply, in just being oneself.

[3] Controlling the "Urdarquelle" is an unidentified maternal goddess, perhaps related to Gaia, since her giant son, Typhon, is also part of the myth (see X, 61 and 65). There is a similar goddess in the mine in *Die Bergwerke zu Falun*.

This "lesson" of the myth is clear enough, as is its *general* application to the story of Giglio and Giacinta. In the beginning they fail to "see" themselves clearly, for they are both preoccupied with extraneous thoughts: Giacinta with her daydreams of wealth and beautiful apparel; and Giglio with his delusions of being first a great tragic actor, then later, Prince Chiapperi. Because of this, "Der Gedanke zerstört die Anschauung." They lack true perception, hence they cannot experience life themselves, nor truly see each other. Only by seeing one another in the "Urdarquelle," in a "humorous" light, whereby their real inner selves become manifest, can they come to know themselves and each other both as "Anschauung" and as "Gedanke," and therefore lead lives rooted in a mythical essence. In addition to the mythical level of meaning, there is a communal one, i.e., Giglio and Giacinta are chosen by Duke Pistoja to act at a theater which performs the function of the "Urdarquelle" for all of Rome, so that a whole society may undergo the same transformation as Giglio and Giacinta. So much for the allegory of the tale.

There is great difficulty at certain points, however, arising from some basic ambiguities of the whole carnival situation. We are confronted by a bewildering fusion of the actual and the imagined. In choosing the carnival as the milieu of the story, Hoffmann uncovered possibilities that were new in his career as a writer, yet peculiarly appropriate for his dualistic world view. For here the starkest actuality is present in closest juxtaposition with the most unrestricted fantasy.

It is a hitherto unrealized fact in critical discussions of this story that the masquerade has a very *real* side to it, in *Prinzessin Brambilla*, as well as in Hoffmann's time, for it was a very common form of entertainment. In *Prinzessin*

Brambilla, there is usually a down-to-earth explanation for every mystery. There is, in the first place, the atmosphere of the carnival season with all the fantastic atmosphere and happenings that recur every year in Roman Catholic areas. Secondly, changing of identities, often with complete concealment of the masked person would be a common occurrence. Also, in connection with the mask identities, it is quite within the natural order of things to play out some fiction associated with these identities, sometimes with foreknowledge of the participants, sometimes without it. Thus the "explanation" for the story could boil down to a *contrivance* on the part of the Duke of Pistoja to reform the Roman theater and, as part of the plan, to cause Giglio and Giacinta to fall in love and to join the Roman comedy. This being the case, Giacinta would have to be acting a good deal of the time in connivance with Pistoja and Bescapi—being absent when Giglio visits her, appearing on the balcony of Bescapi's house and later denying she was there, etc. As for Giglio, his actions would be interpreted largely as willing conformity to the fiction, acting his part as seems to be expected of him. This aspect of the story is irrefutably supported at the end when Pistoja—who has been posing as Celionati—visits Giglio and Giacinta and admits frankly that he had planned it all, and that much of the fantasy was a mere "allegorization" of the meaning of things involved in the plot. Such a contrivance—disregarding its fantastic side—is an extremely common thing in the novel tradition preceding Hoffmann, going back to the *Bundesroman* of the eighteenth century and manifest in the *Bildungsroman* of his time, as in *Wilhelm Meister.*

The contrivance in the story—no matter how real and important it is—does not, however, explain everything.

In the first place, its fantastic elements are far too elaborate for anyone but a divine emissary to manipulate. Also, it is stretching credibility far too much to label as "contrivance" the perfect performance on the part of Giglio and Giacinta throughout the story whenever it is time for them to play the roles of Prince Chiapperi and Princess Brambilla. Their very acceptance of the roles, and their apparent foreknowledge of these other existences have no complete explanation.

Therefore the real contrivance is Hoffmann's—a reason for Celionati's calling the story an "erlogenes Capriccio," and for much of the other irony with which the story abounds. Wherein, then, lies the "reality"—if any—of the mythical area of the story? Any answer would necessarily be based on points where the two realms of the tale join one another. It has already been emphasized that a carnival masquerade provides a juncture area peculiarly suited to Hoffmann's double reality. Nothing in common experience could be more like a Hoffmannesque fantasy than a masquerade.

On this fantastic-realistic border area of his story are certain pivotal points. First and foremost is the contriver, Celionati, being both a wealthy benefactor of eighteenth-century Rome, and a conjurer evoking a primeval mythical world. His friend is Ruffiamonte, the magician of the myth. Then there is Giacinta, the seamstress, who in the myth bears the identity of Princess Mystilis (an alias of Princess Brambilla), whose favorite occupation is also a form of needle work—making netting. As for Giglio, his mythical identity is that of the many-colored bird, the "Gelbschnabel," who must be caught by netting similar to that woven by Mystilis, in order to release her from her enchantment.

These pivotal points between the two stories are accompanied by more subtle correspondences. This is especially true of the story of King Ophioch and Queen Liris, who are the mythical prototypes of Giglio and Giacinta. The development in the story of Ophioch is from sadness to mirth; that of Giglio from tragedy to comedy. King Ophioch's conversion is aided greatly by Liris, who likes to make netting; Giglio's comes about with the assistance of the seamstress Giacinta. In the middle stage of his conversion, Ophioch falls asleep while sadly puzzling over his life; also Giglio falls asleep over one of Chiari's tragedies. And, of course, both achieve their final state of bliss by gazing into the "Urdarquelle."

What is the nature and meaning of these interrelationships? The reality of each of the two worlds represented here is quite different from the other. "Urdargarten" exists in the timeless, always accessible reservoir of myth. Since it is primeval, it is fundamental at all times. The actual world of Rome is elusively fleeting by, with fundamental realities either absent or rejected: Giglio is compared to an empty cardboard mannikin stuffed with the waste paper of Chiari tragedies (X, 110 f.); Giacinta is a capricious and coy daydreamer; the cultural life, reflected in the theater, is bloodless and inane. For life to become genuinely active and fundamentally real, dormant and invisible things must reappear. Thus the myth is an expression of a reality whose potential is always latent in actuality, but must be evoked.

This has a great deal in common with our interpretation of *Der goldne Topf* in Chapter II. There are some important differences, however. In *Prinzessin Brambilla*, the two worlds are inextricably fused and simultaneous with one another in the fantastic actuality of the carnival. This is the crux of the difficulty in interpreting many individual scenes, but also provides a more fully-developed border area where the two come together than in *Der goldne Topf*, in which magic transformation must be resorted to for the transition. Also, in *Der goldne Topf*, Atlantis is primarily the separate world of poetry; whereas Urdargarten is that area of Hoffmann's myth from which all human beings may equally derive renascence by means of a cosmic revivifying force, embodied in a profound form of humor. Finally, there is here an important element almost totally lacking in Anselmus: *Doppelgängertum*. *Prinzessin Brambilla* is Hoffmann's fullest, most analytical treatment of the double personality. For here we have not only the individual character seeing his own double—as in *Die Elixiere des Teufels*—but two characters, Giglio and Giacinta, each seeing his own double *and* that of the other. Thus, much of the course of the story involves an interplay of the four figures: Giacinta and Brambilla, and Giglio and Chiapperi, interacting in various combinations on the basis of varying "Wahlverwandtschaften." And most important of all is the nature of the *Doppelgängertum*. Here we have characters who do not simply have "other" personalities, as in Hoffmann's other *Doppelgänger*, but their doubles are the ideal personalities of the actual characters—what they really are under the surface, and should, and actually do become in their daily lives. Thus *Prinzessin Brambilla* has its roots in both *Der goldne Topf* and *Die Elixiere des Teufels*, and develops further some of the techniques of both, resulting in a highly successful and original accomplishment in characterization.

The work goes beyond personal psychology, however. The allegory of the "Urdarquelle" as representing the comic stage broadens the story's audience to all who might view it: i.e., all mankind. The mythical figures are thus prototypes for all human beings. This does not mean that the story is an allegory: the ironical buffoonery at the end about Celionati's alleged allegorizing deflates the story's potential in this respect far more than it supports it. The myth is a pattern of beautiful images interwoven with a wisdom that is, to be sure, humorously oriented, yet profound. This may involve "meaning" with reference to something else: but then the myth no longer is itself, but a tool for extraneous purposes. Thus Giglio and Giacinta must, in a sense, actually become Chiapperi and Brambilla in order to live their lives to the fullest degree; this is possible only if they live a myth. Here more than any place else does Hoffmann's dictum on allegory apply: "Allegorische Gemälde machen nur Schwächlinge und Stümper. Mein Bild soll nicht *bedeuten*, sondern *sein*." (Said by Berklinger, the artist in *Artushof*, V, 185) With *Prinzessin Brambilla*, Hoffmann created a new province of his poetic kingdom that does not signify, but *is*.

There is a wide gap between *Prinzessin Brambilla* and Hoffmann's last Märchen, *Meister Floh*. Although the latter was begun only a year after *Brambilla*, the differences between the two are sufficient to indicate possibly a totally new trend in Hoffmann's *Märchen*, cut short by his death in 1822, only a few months after the completion of *Meister Floh*. This change in the form and style of Hoffmann's *Märchen* has made it particularly difficult to assess the story justly and clearly. The work has no parallel in ingenious, fantastic inventiveness in certain individual figures and scenes. What could be more unforgettably original than a "master flea," leader of a nation struggling for its freedom; and the person from whom he seeks aid, the childlike Peregrinus Tyss, a recluse afraid of women in actuality, but "in reality" King Sekakis, husband of the Flower Queen? And there is the whimsical invention of Meister Floh's miniature microscope that enables Tyss to read other people's thoughts. Few of Hoffmann's feminine figures—with the exception of Serpentina—are more tantalizing than the lithesome Dörtje Elverdink alias Aline the younger, alias Princess Gamaheh, alias the Yellow and Purple Tulip. The figure of Tyss' friend, the problematical Georg Pepusch, is one of Hoffmann's most successfully drawn eccentrics, with his essential character magnificently symbolized in his mythical "other identity," that of the thistle Zeherit, lover of the tulip Gamaheh. Original to a surrealistic extreme is the pair Thetel and Egel ("Leech"), the one flying about the inn at will and the other changing his proportions from tall and thin to short and squat. Finally, who but Hoffmann at his best would have thought of having the petty scientists Leuwenhoek and Swammerdamm fight a fencing duel with stinging beams of light coming from telescopes? All these things are worthy of the high quality of the overall plot of the story itself, in which a large group of persons find their "true" identities in a mythical plant world.

In spite of this magnificent fantastic inventiveness, the story has astonishing flaws, of which Hoffmann, in a major work, would be capable only under the pressure of the extreme illness and worry that burdened him during its writing.[4] Moreover, he did not have a large part of the manuscript of the first half (which was at his publishers) to refer to while writing the second half, thus causing sev-

[4] See von Müller's *Nachwort zu Meister Floh* in his edition of the text of the work (Berlin, 1900), p. 231 ff.

eral serious contradictions. Hans von Müller lists the
more important of those details occurring in the first half
which Hoffmann overlooked toward the end of the story.[5]

One could go beyond individual details, and find some
rather weak points in the overall plot. Why, for example,
did Hoffmann go to all the trouble of creating the love
affair between Peregrinus and Dörtje, only to pair them off
later to other mates (Röschen and Pepusch), who help
them to recover their true mythical identities? Why not
let Dörtje be the "Blumenkönigin," Peregrinus' soul-mate
in his Sekakis identity? Why does he suddenly create a
new character (the simple, down-to-earth Röschen Läm-
merhirt) out of nowhere in the very last chapter to play
the role of the Flower Queen in the final scene? There is
an answer of sorts to this question, but it gives rise to
great bewilderment in other respects: namely, that Peregrinus cannot marry Dörtje because in the myth she is
his daughter—a fact that is generally overlooked. Dörtje
is Princess Gamaheh, who is the daughter of King Sekakis,
and he is identical with Peregrinus Tyss! Moreover (and
this involves great contradiction with the outcome of the
last chapter) Aline the Elder, Peregrinus' phenomenally
ugly housekeeper, could at one point very well be the
mother of Aline the Younger; hence she would be Peregrinus' spouse of the mythical realm! This is suggested by
four facts (1) Naming the two characters "Aline," as
Hoffmann did in other works with persons in different
generations of the same family (e.g., *Die Elixiere des
Teufels* and *Das Majorat*). The relationship of the two
is strongly suggested at one point, where Aline I enters

---

[5] Von Müller, *op. cit.* p. 243 ff. Harich claims (II, 352 f.) that von Müller
overemphasized these details, and failed to see a certain unity. My view
lies somewhere between these two.

the room and Peregrinus senses the presence of Aline II
(X, 178). (2) The emotional ties between the two Alines,
coupled with an unexplained reference to some previous
close relationship. I refer to the passage in which Aline I
is about to explain to Tyss what Aline II had recognized
in her, then refuses to go on (X, 213: 27 ff.). That Aline I
is her mother is the logical explanation. Aline II also says
that Aline I has "found her mother" at Tyss' house (X,
211: 36). This is undoubtedly meant primarily as a figure
of speech in this context, yet can also be literally true.
(3) The motherly care which Aline I, in her mythical
identity as the "Mandragora" root, has bestowed upon
Princess Gamaheh as she lay "dead" (157: 4 ff.). (4) There
is a similar combination of characters in the story *Datura
Fastuosa*, Hoffmann's *Vorstudie* for *Meister Floh*. Here
a young man (Eugenius), marries an elderly woman (the
"Frau Professorin"), who has a step-daughter (Gretchen)
with whom Eugenius falls in love. Aline I's delusion of
Tyss' forthcoming marriage with Aline II (X, 214) further substantiates the parallel. These relationships cannot,
however, fit into the story as it evolves toward its conclusion. Therefore Hoffmann cuts these ties without further ado for the sake of the Peregrinus-Röschen and
Zeherit-Gamaheh stories, and then to Aline I is ascribed
the mythical identity of the Queen of Golkonda.

This is all part of a general looseness in the whole
structure and progression of the story. The prime example
of this is the Knarrpanti episodes, which, to say the least,
constitute a digression. And it seems to be almost a studied
incoherency where Hoffmann tells the mildly amusing,
but pointless anecdote, "Geschichte des Schneiderleins aus
Sachsenhausen." It would be easy to multiply further this
list of contradictions and irrelevancies.

To be sure, one can dismiss the story as an unsuccessful experiment due to the unfavorable conditions under which it was written. There is more to it than this, however, for there are definite symptoms of a new phase in Hoffmann's literary art. This is best demonstrated by an examination of the background myth.

There are certain important mythical features that *Meister Floh* has in common with stories such as *Der goldne Topf* and *Prinzessin Brambilla*. The background myth is rooted in primeval times; this myth breaks through the reality of modern actuality, thereby deepening and revitalizing certain favored characters; *Doppelgängertum* (*Prinzessin Brambilla*) is further developed; and one could point out innumerable common figures and motifs.

There is, however, a major shift of emphasis in the basic myth from the animal and mineral, to the vegetable kingdom. Although plant life is certainly nothing new in Hoffmann's basic myths—the "Feuerlilie" in *Der goldne Topf*, the "Lotosblume" in *Prinzessin Brambilla*, and the whole bulbous retinue of Daucus Carota I in *Königsbraut*, to mention a few instances—but such motifs generally were not central. There were some definite signs of this new development in Hoffmann's writings coming shortly before *Meister Floh*. Hoffmann had planned a "botanical novella" at the suggestion of Chamisso.[6] Then comes the aforementioned *Datura fastuosa*, which was clearly a step in the direction of *Meister Floh* in its horticultural atmosphere. But not until *Meister Floh* does Hoffmann bestow on human life and its world the laws of the growth of flowers and trees in mythical realms. Previous to this, the life of the mythical world and its extensions into actuality

6 *Briefwechsel*, II, 2, p. 295 f.

are charged mainly with the dynamic, fiery energy of the Salamander: now the common denominator of all life is the scarcely perceptible, but inexorable power of unconscious organic growth.

The childlike main character, Peregrinus Tyss, is appropriate for such a story, because the unconscious processes involved here presuppose the lack of aggressive, analytical intelligence. Hoffmann goes to extremes here. Tyss is no mere clumsy Anselmus; for Peregrinus' childlikeness occasionally deteriorates into plain imbecility. But, as in Dostoevsky's *Idiot*, these extremes are necessary in such conceptions of a sharply divided humanity and world. The essential actions must ultimately be grounded in a subconscious stratum that is of such transcendent wisdom and beauty that it would be a mockery to apply ordinary human intelligence. Hence, an apparent imbecility in the everyday world is highly appropriate here. This situation—an imbecile being acted upon, unbeknown to him, by transcendent cosmic powers in an empty world—remains essentially the same up to the very end of the story.

The plant-like growth and development of the cosmos is regarded as foreign to modern actuality. Peregrinus' world of nineteenth-century Frankfurt is seen as illusory and superficial. The magic eyeglass enabling him to read the minds of people on the streets demonstrates this. Those persons who are supposedly engaged in attempting to penetrate nature through science (Leuwenhoek and Swammerdamm) can only make a colossal mess of things. They are guilty of keeping the Tulip Princess Gamaheh (as Dörtje) mentally and physically removed from her natural habitat in timeless Famagusta. Their talent at being utterly wrong demonstrates itself at the most critical junctures: they do not know that it is actually Meister

Floh who has brought Gamaheh to life, and their mis-interpretation of Peregrinus' horoscope is as complete as it can be. Worse than this is their humiliation and defile-ment of the creatures of nature. Not only is Dörtje a captive, but also a whole "race" of creatures: the flea-people of Meister Floh.

It cannot be denied that Hoffmann's title for this tale is misleading: it is not really about Meister Floh. Yet there is some justification in drawing the reader's attention to him, in that his role is pivotal for the various characters and milieus of the tale. (One might compare it with changing the title of Goethe's *Faust* to *Mephistopheles*.) Meister Floh's origin is the mythical world, yet he is a captive in the real one, and is involved in the realities of both. He, like Mephistopheles, serves as an instrument of a higher reality to act both in connection with this reality and with the world. Unlike Mephistopheles, however, he really does not belong in the world, but in the myth of his origin. He is victimized by the exploiters of nature.

These exploiters, Leuwenhoek and Swammerdamm, have something in common with other "scientists" in Hoff-mann's tales, notably Mosch Terpin in *Klein Zaches*, a petty type of analytical mind that thinks that he is pene-trating into nature's secrets by fussing over trivialities. These "wahnsinnige Detailhändler der Natur" (X, 258) are condemned in a manner resembling the punishment of the sinners in Dante's *Inferno*: the penalty is made reminiscent of the transgression in that they become childish, obedient little doll figures, analogous to what they had hoped to make of Dörtje, Meister Floh, and the flea people.

The ultimate victory of nature (along with the myth embodying it) is not achieved without sacrifice. Here we have a justification for the sub-plot of Gamaheh and Zeherit. The hero, Peregrinus, manages to achieve his mythical, natural identity without giving up his existence in the world. This is not true of the lesser spirits. They cannot, after marriage, continue to live both actually and mythically as do Peregrinus and Röschen. Perhaps Dörtje Elverdink and Georg Pepusch are not sufficiently human to do this. Dörtje's mythical identity as a colorful and lithesome tulip, and Georg's mythical character as a prickly, temperamental thistle are too close to the surface for them to achieve full humanity. Thus in the overall attainment of harmony and balance between myth and life in this story, Dörtje and Georg must be sacrificial lambs. It is assumed, however, that they maintain a certain potential to come to life again, for they have died the "Blumentod," which Dörtje has already suffered and from which she has hitherto been revived. In their "death" they can be regarded as symbolic of the world of myth that is often absent, but can be resurrected. Peregrinus achieves full existence in myth and in actuality by virtue of the "carbuncle," a double symbol of his human heart and his deep-rooted identity as King Sekakis in Famagusta. Unlike objects of the subterranean *niveaux* in other stories by Hoffmann (especially *Die Bergwerke zu Falun*) the carbuncle is not a demonic emblem: on the contrary, its essence is one of vitality and light—attributes of the "upper world" of *Der goldne Topf*.

We therefore can see in *Meister Floh* considerable modification of Hoffmann's mythical world. The major shift of emphasis from animal and mineral images to those of plants reflects a shift in connotations. No longer does myth explosively break through into life, but it slowly and powerfully asserts itself by becoming imperceptibly intertwined into life, changing it gently, as always with organic growth, until the world of actuality cannot help but blend with it, as when Peregrinus and Röschen, like Giglio and Giacinta, marry in both their real and their ideal identities. The eternity of such identities is symbolized as nowhere else in Hoffmann by forces sleeping in a "Blumentod," actually a form of immortality.

It is, in a way, appropriate that Hoffmann's explorations and creations in the world of myth should end with *Meister Floh*, for this story casts a fixed and timeless light on his other realms of *Märchenmythos*. It must be emphasized that there is no real discrepancy between these realms; the various stories emphasize, from different perspectives, the diverse sides of his Romantic mythology. In retrospect, however, *Meister Floh* helps to stabilize and provide a firmer foundation for the dynamic, sometimes over-creative areas of his mythology, as in the extreme, dynamic, almost chaotic creativity of *Der goldne Topf*.

With ever-growing maturity—coupled, paradoxically, with an increasing penchant for the childlike—Hoffmann explored myth with ever greater directness of vision, at the same time increasing its profundity and complexity. It is no accident that three of the tales are primarily children's tales (*Nussknacker und Mausekönig, Das fremde Kind, Die Königsbraut*); but hand-in-hand with this ingenuous directness are the extreme complexity and bearing on adult life in *Klein Zaches* and *Prinzessin Brambilla*. We cannot know how much further the new direction of *Meister Floh* might have taken him. As it is, we have a series of eight stories, leading us through an imaginative realm that is equalled by few other fantastic poetic worlds in originality and grandeur.

9

Lebensansichten des Katers Murr

No discussion of Hoffmann's tales is complete without considering *Kater Murr*, his unfinished last novel. Although it is not mythical in the same sense as are the works discussed in the last two chapters, yet it is completely relevant here, for Hoffmann's mythology operates under the surface of this work in a way that is revealing for some of the obscure areas in this puzzling novel, for the direction that his literary art was taking, and for the subsequent realistic direction in nineteenth-century German literature.

Extremely difficult questions are posed by this work. We must first come to terms with the frequently interrupted, often bewildering double narrative of the hilarious biography of a tom-cat and the sombre, tragic tale of Johannes Kreisler. Also, we are hampered by the fact that Hoffmann did not complete the novel, leaving many mysteries of Kreisler's background unsolved. It is like *Die Elixiere des Teufels* with its episodes broken apart, then shuffled like playing cards, omitting in the process the manuscript of the old painter. Some ingenious attempts have been made to create the missing pieces of the puzzle, but they have been largely concerned with merely establishing the family relationships.[1]

Yet even in its incomplete form, *Kater Murr* remains Hoffmann's most original single accomplishment with respect to structure. In spite of the many frustrating blank areas left in our total image of the work, it remains a magnificent symphony of characters, milieus, and moods on various levels. A virtuosity not unlike that of an orchestra director, keeping track of all the individual instruments and parts of the musical composition, is here in evidence.

Outstanding in originality is the double narrative form itself. There are widely diverging views on this matter among Hoffmann scholars. Hans von Müller published the Kreisler and the Murr sections separately, for he considered the Murr episodes to be an unfortunate whim, stemming from downright pathological tendencies in Hoffmann: "Ich kann freilich in dieser Verbindung nur eine krankhafte Roheit sehen. . . . Das kranke Gemüth greift zu perversen Stimulantien. . . ."[2] Contrast this with Gustav Egli's appraisal of the work: ". . . es bedeutet . . . eine unbegreifliche Verkennung von Hoffmanns künstlerischer Absicht, Katerbiographie und Kreislerfragmente gesondert herauszugeben . . . Nur in ihrer Zusammenstellung mit der Schönheit der Kreislerfragmente enthüllt sich der ganze Zynismus in Murrs erbärmlicher literarischer Mache—nur in ihr wird aber auch das Lächeln des versöhnenden

[1] Harich, II, 233; Willimczik, p. 272f.
[2] Hans von Müller, *Das Kreislerbuch* (Leipzig, 1903) p. XLIV f.

Humors offenbar, das dem ganzen Werke erst die letzte
Weihe und seine eigentliche Schönheit gibt."[3]

Judging by Hoffmann's other works, one would expect
the two worlds—represented by the two sets of fragments—
to be the mythical and the actual. Here this is definitely
not the case. Although Kreisler's biography takes place
in the common everyday world, and is more or less
realistically oriented, the "other world" of Murr's autobiography is in no way the primeval mythical realm of
Der goldne Topf. Although giving a cat human attributes
is a product of the author's fancy, essentially the everyday
world is depicted here also. Murr is a surrealistic satire of
the Philistine type of human being who is so often mocked
in Hoffmann's tales. By putting such a character on the
lower level of the beast (thus creating, in a way, a new
kind of *Bildungsphilister* underworld!), the Philistine is
made to appear all the more absurd. The absurdity is
multiplied when Murr frequently elevates himself to the
sublime regions of lyric poetry and philosophical idealism,
only to descend in the same breath to the lowest level of
carnal appetites. He is the supreme satirical representation
of the social forces opposing Kreisler, for Murr embodies
the Philistine mentality in its lowest form, set off in sharp
contrast to the sublimity of Hoffmann's concept of music,
"die romantischste aller Künste."

Murr's world, then, is not really an "other world," but
a satirical representation of actuality. The myth must be
sought elsewhere if there is one. Myth definitely does not
enter the work in the same dramatic way as in the beginning of the third *Vigilie* of *Der goldne Topf.* Nothing
remotely resembling "Atlantis" seems to be present here.
Yet there are a great many isolated factors paralleling *Der*

[3] Egli, p. 117.

goldne Topf and other mythical tales, hinting at a transcendent level of meaning for the largely realistic Kreisler story.

The outstanding example is Meister Abraham's "unsichtbares Mädchen," who seems to possess supernatural qualities, and with whom he appears to be in telepathic contact (IX, 316 ff.). The bell tones announcing her are similar to those introducing Serpentina to Anselmus. In fact, wherever Meister Abraham appears, there is generally something in the scene that clearly points beyond common experience, and indicates his power over his environment. This is typical of all of Hoffmann's master figures. Can we then identify him with Lindhorst, the most fully developed of the master figures?

There are indeed striking parallels. Like Archivarius Lindhorst, Abraham is not merely a "master" of his craft (in this case organ-builder and *maitre de plaisir*), but a master in all situations. His power of leadership is demonstrated in his relationship with every major character. He even masters another "master," "Kapellmeister" Kreisler, whose almost filial relationship with Abraham is comparable to that of Anselmus with Lindhorst. This power approaches the uncanny, and finds its most appropriate symbolic representation in Abraham's activities as a court magician who is especially gifted in creating optical and auditory illusions. This has its parallel in Lindhorst's "magic trick" whereby he lights a pipe with a snap of his fingers.

This leads us to the most remarkable parallel: Meister Abraham is also repeatedly associated with fire—both actual and figurative. In the *Namenstag* celebration at the beginning of the novel, he dramatically unleashes his fire to illuminate the ludicrous chaos of the event. Later, when

his apartment is about to burn, he is singularly uncon-
cerned about it all, as if he were in control; and it turns
out that the danger is far less than it appears at first. These
two actual fires are externalizations of certain underlying
forces that, like this element itself, can either nourish or
consume. In the very scene in which Abraham tells of the
fire at the *Namenstag* celebration, he transforms actual
flames into a metaphor while chastizing Kreisler: "Wilder
unbesonnener Mensch . . . wann wird endlich der ver-
wüstende Brand in deiner Brust zur reinen Naphtha-
flamme werden, genährt von dem tiefsten Sinn für die
Kunst, für alles Herrliche und Schöne, der in dir wohnt!"
(IX, 35.) The metaphor here implies that mastery over
fire is emblematic of mastery over life. Such power is
"elemental," and is derived from the *Urwelt* of Hoffmann's myths. Therefore Abraham is, in a sense, a de-
scendant of the elemental spirits of fire, the salamanders,
and hence a blood brother of Lindhorst. Of course it
must be admitted that Hoffmann makes no mention of
this worthy provenance in his novel. Yet, in view of the
parallel roles and emblems assigned to Lindhorst and
Abraham, one can come to no other conclusion but that a
mythical realm is indirectly asserting itself through Abraham, and providing a depth and sense of the primal
throughout the novel. For he is a pivotal character whose
presence is felt amidst all the diverse tensions of the story.

Kreisler's tragic flaw, as suggested in the above quotation, lies in his inability to discipline his "fire"—which in
Abraham's admonishment is restricted to the meaning of
the driving force of the artist. This elemental power is
creative when kept pure and restrained, and is destructive
when it rages out of control. As Abraham claims, Kreisler's
"fire" has indeed the latter tendency, and bursts forth at
one point in a way that makes the full meaning of the fire

emblem for Kreisler unmistakably clear. This occurs at the concert when Kreisler and Julia sing a duet, and it appears that he has allowed the "Naphthaflamme" of his art to ignite rather than only to illumine; for Hedwiga is deeply disturbed by the alleged extravagance of Kreisler's music. The mocking irony of his "apology" to Hedwiga turns into almost hysterical buffoonery as Kreisler apparently senses more and more, while speaking, the danger that he poses: "ich habe schändlich gefrevelt mit dem entsetzlichen Duett, das wie ein höllisches Feuerwerk mit allerlei Leuchtkugeln, Schwanzraketen, Schwärmern und Kanonenschlägen durch die ganze Gesellschaft gefahren ist und, leider merk' ich's, fast überall gezündet hat!— Ha!—Feuer—Feuer—Mordio!—es brennt—Spritzenhaus auf —Wasser—Wasser—Hilfe, rettet!" (IX, 129 f.) The effect of this outburst is heightened by its close juxtaposition to an actual fire—the above-mentioned one, which is burning in the vicinity of Meister Abraham's quarters, and which the "master" seems to have under control by his mere presence (IX, 122 and 132).

It is apparent that this fire imagery has positive and negative forms, representing, as will be seen, conflicting forces between which a life-and-death struggle is taking place, to a large degree under the surface of the novel. With respect to Kreisler, this battle is being fought between those persons desiring to maintain the "Naphtha-flamme" of art, and those who would cause or allow this fire to burst its bonds. More than art, however, is involved. "Fire" is also emblematic of a more fundamental living force; and the two opposing camps—led by Abraham and Rätin Benzon—represent two ways of life hostile to one another: the disciplined and creative versus the uncontrollably impassioned and destructive. This all becomes more apparent when we observe other main characters.

The destructive forces emanate from Rätin Benzon, who is Abraham's evil feminine counterpart, and as such suggestive of a witch figure, such as Liese, the avowed foe of Lindhorst. Therefore it is of primary significance for Benzon's relation to the myth that Abraham applies the fire image to her in the following way: "... arme unglückliche Frau! Ruhe, Zufriedenheit vermeinst du gewonnen zu haben und ahndest nicht, dass es die Verzweiflung war, die, *ein Vulkan, alle flammende Gluten aus deinem Innern hinausströmen liess,* und dass du nun die tote Asche, aus der keine Blüte, keine Blume mehr sprosst, in starrer Betörung für das reiche Feld des Lebens hältst, das dir noch Früchte spenden soll." (IX, 209; italics mine) These metaphors contain a mythical figuration, closely resembling that in the struggle of the upper and lower forces in the very beginning of the myth in *Der goldne Topf,* where the dark depths send forth deadly vapors to prevent the sun from nourishing the flowers ("Aus den Abgründen rollten die Dünste empor ..." I, 189). Thus, through imagery, Rätin Benzon is labelled with a mythical emblem placing her ultimate origin in the underworld.

In league with Rätin Benzon is Prince Hektor, a Neapolitan officer and one of Hoffmann's most sinister satanic figures. It is volcanic fire, like Rätin Benzon's, to which he is drawn, for when he sees Hedwiga, whom eventually he is to marry, he says: "Sie ist schön, aber unfern des Vesuvs geboren, und sein Feuer blitzt aus ihren Augen." (IX, 169)[4] Hektor himself is compared

---

[4] This suggests an interesting dimension to Hedwiga's neurotic and mysterious personality; aside from this comment, there is no reason to associate her with the underworld, except as its victim. Both Harich and Willimczik (see note 1) claim that she is the daughter of Abraham and Chiara—a strange choice of parents, in view of their idealized love relationship, for such a problematical daughter.

with fearsome animal creatures, which are apparently related to such underworld monsters as Liese's forebear, the black dragon. On a single page Hektor is described as a *mostro turchino*, like that in a Gozzi play of the same title, a dragon, and a basilisk (IX, 172). A few pages later Hedwiga, who is still suffering from the shock of the encounter with him, adds one more variation to this imagery when she tells of a dream in which she is attacked by a vampire (IX, 176). Thus Hektor's demonic nature is made unmistakably clear by reference to Hoffmann's underworld.

To extend the parallels with *Der goldne Topf* unreservedly to Julia would be unjustified, for her resemblance to either Serpentina or Veronika is slight. Yet she too evokes some associations with the mythical—although not in the same way as the other characters. Julia is one of Hoffmann's idealized feminine figures, and as such is representative of the "other world" of music, which is not clearly integrated into the myth of *Der goldne Topf*. She comprises a more or less separate and deeply personal myth, like the Julia of the earlier Kreisler fragments discussed in Chapters One and Three. At one point in the novel, she is unmistakably elevated into this supra-human realm by a dream in which she finds herself in an idyllic garden—much like Atlantis—and discovers that she is not really a person, but a melody that was wandering through the air of the garden (IX, 173). Only in a general sense, then, can Julia be equated with Serpentina, in that both have "other-worldly" features (the latter much more, of course), and both are associated with an aethereal kind of music.

In drawing such parallels, the point must be stressed that Julia, as well as all the other persons discussed above,

are in no sense portrayed by Hoffmann as having direct
ties with his mythical world. There is not a single mention of such connections, nor any revelation of a realm
such as "Atlantis," "Urdargarten," "Dschinnistan," and
the like. Abraham, Benzon, Hektor, and Julia merely
bear *emblems* of Hoffmann's myth, and Kreisler is shown
to be indirectly influenced by it, thus elevating actuality
toward a mythical level. Thus the sharp dichotomy between myth and actuality, as in *Der goldne Topf*, is not
present here: myth is subtly blended into the everyday
world so that the world as we know it shows a potentiality
of transformation into a world rooted in mythical origins,
and operating according to the natural primeval laws implicit in Hoffmann's conception of the world's creation.
Hoffmann "romanticizes" the world in the special sense
formulated by Novalis in his often cited fragment: "Die
Welt muss romantisiert werden. So findet man den ur-
sprünglichen Sinn wieder. Romantisieren ist nichts als
eine qualitative Potenzierung. Das niedre Selbst wird mit
einem bessern Selbst in dieser Operation identifiziert . . .
Indem ich dem Gemeinen einen hohen Sinn, dem Ge-
wöhnlichen ein geheimnisvolles Ansehn, dem Bekannten
die Würde des Unbekannten, dem Endlichen einen unendlichen Schein gebe, so romantisiere ich es. . . ." (Fragment no. 1921.)

Hoffmann did not carry this mythologizing process as
far as he could have in the completed sections of the novel,
and it seems doubtful that he would have done so—by
adding, for example, a purely mythical section toward the
end. In the first place, such sections are usually introduced
toward the beginning of the story (as in *Der goldne Topf*
and *Prinzessin Brambilla*), and form points of departure
for the remainder of the story. Secondly, another "ro-

manticizing" process along the lines of Novalis' fragment largely supplants the mythical kind—namely, the pervading of actuality with the mysteries of unknown family relationships, as in *Die Elixiere des Teufels.*

Nonetheless, the mythical emblems in the Kreisler story greatly enrich it; and Hoffmann's Romantic myth is a perceptible, though remote, part of its total artistry.

10

Conclusion

From the foregoing eight chapters, it is apparent that Hoffmann produced a personal mythology that bore some of the major features of Friedrich Schlegel's concept of a new mythology. There is a coherent body of myth in Hoffmann's world of fantasy from which poetic materials are derived for all of his literary works. Its function is, in general, that of an "Urquell" and "Mittelpunkt" for the poetic in all of his tales. This mythology is concentrated mainly in the four major *Märchenmythen* in *Der goldne Topf, Klein Zaches, Prinzessin Brambilla,* and *Meister Floh.* These can be supplemented by the lesser myths in *Ritter Gluck, Die Elixiere des Teufels, Der Sandmann, Nussknacker und Mausekönig, Das fremde Kind,* and *Die Königsbraut.*

If we are to accept any single myth as the fundamental one in Hoffmann, it would be the one contained in the first few pages of the third *Vigilie* in *Der goldne Topf,* for it is the most primeval and has the greatest potential of further development. This myth, in a few respects, is ". . . selbst das unendliche Gedicht, welches die Keime aller andern Gedichte verhüllte," especially if applied only to its function in the totality of Hoffmann's works, and not to those of any other authors. Its fundamental nature is apparent from its origins in the Creation itself, and it weaves a broad tapestry of the *Urzeit*, which comprises the essence of Hoffmann's mythology. Hoffmann himself did not make any statements clearly defining this function of *Der goldne Topf* in the totality of his literary achievement, nor did he clearly express an intention to create such a standard myth. He did, however, clearly indicate his belief in the superiority of *Der goldne Topf* when he wrote in a letter to Hippel: "Ich schreibe keinen goldnen Topf mehr!—So was muss man nur recht lebhaft fühlen und sich selbst keine Illusion machen." (Aug. 30, 1816.) The extent to which the myth of this one work can be used as source for the interpretation of other works has been demonstrated in the many references I have made to *Der goldne Topf* throughout this book.

Yet this mythical world undergoes some modification in works written both before and after *Der goldne Topf*. The three realms of Ritter Gluck's imaginative world are different from the three realms in Lindhorst's; yet the two are not altogether incompatible with each other. The "Urdarquelle" (*Prinzessin Brambilla*) is a totally new feature of the *Urzeit* as previously portrayed. And in *Meister Floh*, the whole vigorously dynamic quality of the myth in *Der goldne Topf* is transformed into a slow and calm, but inexorable organic development, symbolized by plant-growth.

A part of the myth in *Der goldne Topf* does, however, comprise unreservedly "das unendliche Gedicht, welches

die Keime aller andern Gedichte verhüllt." This is Hoffmann's version of the Creation: "Der Geist schaute auf
das Wasser, da bewegte es sich und brauste in schäumenden Wogen und stürzte sich donnernd in die Abgründe, die ihren schwarzen Rachen aufsperrten, es gierig
zu verschlingen. Wie triumphierende Sieger hoben die
Granitfelsen ihre zackicht gekrönten Häupter empor, das
Tal schützend bis es die Sonne in ihren mütterlichen
Schoss nahm und, es umfassend, mit ihren Strahlen wie
mit glühenden Armen pflegte und wärmte." Hoffmann's
whole mythology, hence everything poetic in his works,
can be derived from this basic figure of conflict between
creative and destructive forces in a middle realm. This
"Urquell," in fact, could have been made the starting
point even for the three main examples of departures from
his myth given above. Ritter Gluck's vision is not one
of the Creation, but takes place at a more advanced stage
of the world; and it includes demons of the depths, a
middle realm of the artist, and the higher creative realm
of the truth, "the sun." The "Urdarquelle," is haunted
by a demon, "Typhon"; it is located in an intermediate,
creative realm; and it is likewise brightened by light. The
slower action of cosmic forces in *Meister Floh* is only a
matter of degree; and its greater attention to plant-life
involves merely a shift of emphasis. Thus, however brief
it may be, Hoffmann's version of the Creation still provides an "Urquell" and "Mittelpunkt." It is obvious that
Schlegel had hoped for something more suitable for a
generally accepted mythology than this; yet his wish is
fulfilled insofar as the myth of *Der goldne Topf* provides
a central source for Hoffmann's own poetic art.

There are, of course, some aspects of Hoffmann's works
that are more remote from his basic myth than others. In

the first place, he sometimes was drawn more toward the underworld, the *Abgründe*, than its original role in the triadic harmony of the *Urzeit* would justify. Tales of the satanic and the underworld nevertheless become a category unto themselves, united in a coherently developed night symbolism. Although the figures and realms of such tales are derivable from the *Abgründe*, they often, in individual tales, remain unrelated to other cosmic forces: i.e., the powers of light and of earthly productivity (the middle realm) with which they originally formed cosmic, creative action. Furthermore there is often in the demonic tales an element that might be called a "myth substitute." This is the ancestral background story that is not a cosmic primeval myth, but operates in the same general way, in that it provides a hitherto invisible force which obtrudes into actuality, as in *Die Elixiere des Teufels, Das Majorat,* and *Kater Murr.*

Hoffmann's many tales of various types of artists are also comparatively remote from the central myth. Their primary relationship to it is a technical one: they seek and develop means of expression for the myth from the arts of music, painting, and of writing itself; and also treat the problems of the artist in society. Only in a few of these stories does the myth assert itself with much power.

There is a definite trend toward the end of Hoffmann's life whereby he came to utilize his myth more and more as part of the fabric of everyday life, with which it had formerly come into violent conflict. The highest point in this development is *Kater Murr*, in which he uses many images having the same connotations as in his myth, but does not explicitly indicate his mythology as its source. This is also true of other major works having strong realistic tendencies, such as *Das Fräulein von Scuderi* and *Das Majorat*. Hoffmann relocated more and more of the mythical *Urzeit* into common experience in his last few years. Life took on more and more attributes of myth, and the violent clashes between myth and actuality were greatly softened. Had he lived longer, he might have developed a primarily realistic literary art, into which his mythical world would have been completely absorbed.

It has been emphasized that the concept of "new mythology" as the source and center of the poetic applies to the whole body of Hoffmann's works. Did it live after Hoffmann, providing in any sense a new mythology for his contemporaries and literary progeny? The answer is apparent to anyone having only a passing acquaintance with subsequent literary history: it definitely did not. The German writers following him hardly attributed such stature to him, although several read and admired him (Heine, Otto Ludwig, Hebbel, Grillparzer, Stifter, Keller). Among those outside Germany who considered him to be a major writer (Pushkin, Gogol, Dostoevski, Baudelaire, R. L. Stevenson, Poe, and many others), there is little evidence that they utilized his works as myth sources, in spite of the deep impression that he made on them in other ways.[1]

An especially revealing case is Dostoevski's, the greatest author among those in the nineteenth century who were deeply influenced by Hoffmann, as Charles Passage has shown with great thoroughness.[2] It was not *Der goldne Topf*—nor any other work containing a *Märchenmythos*—

[1] The extent and nature of Hoffmann's influence on subsequent writers (mainly outside Germany) can be readily seen in Goedeke's *Grundriss*, 8. Buch, 7. Abteilung, 446-454.

[2] Charles Passage, *Dostoevski the Adapter* (Chapel Hill, 1954), esp. p. 136f. and 175ff.

that provided the most materials and stimulation for Dostoevski's major works, but rather *Die Elixiere des Teufels*, in which the religious, psychological, and realistic factors—not the mythical—are the common ground between the two authors. Only in a remote way did Hoffmann create a "new mythology" for anyone but himself, in that many figures, images, motifs, and perhaps some of his world view entered perceptibly into some major works of the nineteenth century, which, in turn, are still influencing us.

Such a mythology as Hoffmann's entails the disadvantage that it is not common knowledge of informed readers, as is the Greek and Roman mythology. Therefore to gain the fullest possible understanding and appreciation of Hoffmann's works, a special learning process is required—its simplest form being an intense reading of *Der goldne Topf* before going on to the others. This in no way denies the artistic autonomy of individual tales. It involves merely a process of orientation for individual themes and their bearing on a total artistic world and vocabulary—a process comparable to studying ancient mythology for the purpose of the fullest possible reading of Homer or Virgil.

In addition, Hoffmann's myths can, of course, be traced to many different sources among the philosophies and literary works of his contemporaries and predecessors; and much is brought to light thereby. In this book, however, I have consciously avoided this approach, with a few exceptions, not only because it would have entailed much needless repetition of the work of others, but—more important—it would have contradicted a basic presupposition. For in properly applying the Romantic idea of a "new mythology," the fundamental question is not from where a given myth comes, but to where it leads. To establish that Hoffmann's basic mythical figuration, as proposed above, is a combination of images and ideas found in, for example, the Book of Genesis, Jakob Böhme, Novalis, and Gotthilf Heinrich von Schubert is largely a true and useful finding. It is not sufficient, however, for an appraisal of Hoffmann's utilization of these sources; for there are many important differences from them, and they often outweigh the similarities. Hoffmann's accomplishment with regard to the sources is, then, not a matter of a successfully wrought eclecticism, but of his shaping from sources a dynamic mythical organism which, after its conception, has the appearance of moving under its own power and of creating an artistic world that embodies fundamental realities in fantastic form. Therefore instead of devoting much attention to the *sources* of Hoffmann's myth, I have regarded it as a source in itself (as proposed by Schlegel), and have inquired into the *products* that it generated.

Approached in this way Hoffmann's works can become a unique literary adventure, untarnished by any worn-out tags and epithets of the commonly known, ancient mythologies, yet having much of their cosmic import. Furthermore, the intensely personal nature of his "new mythology" endows it with the intimate communicability of a confession. Thus we can explore the world in a unique way by means of an individual creative imagination which reveals the often invisible truths and beauties on which the world is founded.

Selected Bibliography

I. Hoffmann's Collected Works, Letters, and Diaries.

E. T. A. Hoffmann, *Werke*, ed. G. Ellinger, 2nd ed. (Berlin-Leipzig, n. d. [1927]).

E. T. A. Hoffmann, *Sämtliche Werke: Historisch-kritische Ausgabe*, ed. C. G. von Maassen (München und Leipzig, 1908-1928).

E. T. A. Hoffmann im persönlichen und brieflichen Verkehr: Sein Briefwechsel und die Erinnerungen seiner Bekannten, ed. von Müller (Berlin, 1912).

E. T. A. Hoffmann, *Tagebücher und literarische Entwürfe*, ed. von Müller (Berlin, 1915).

II. Selected Works Relating to Hoffmann and "New Mythology."

Behler, Ernst, "Friedrich Schlegels Theorie der Universalpoesie," *Jahrbuch der deutschen Schiller-Gesellschaft*, I (1947), 211-252.

Böckmann, Paul, "Die romantische Poesie Brentanos und ihre Grundlagen bei Friedrich Schlegel und Tieck," *Jahrbuch des Freien Deutschen Hochstifts,* MCMXXXIV/V, 56-173.

Bollnow, Otto Friedrich, "Der 'Goldene Topf' und die Naturphilosophie der Romantik," in *Unruhe und Geborgenheit* (Stuttgart, 1953), pp. 207-226.

Bruning, Peter, "E. T. A. Hoffmann and the Philistine," *German Quarterly,* XXVIII (1955), 111-121.

Dahmen, Hans, *E. T. A. Hoffmanns Weltanschauung* (Marburg, 1929).

Dieckmann, Liselotte, "Friedrich Schlegel and Romantic Concepts of the Symbol," *Germanic Review,* XXXIV (1959), 276-283.

Egli, Gustav, *E. T. A. Hoffmann: Ewigkeit und Endlichkeit in seinem Werk* (Zürich-Leipzig-Berlin, 1927).

Floeck, Oswald, *Die Elementargeister bei Fouqué und anderen Dichtern der romantischen und nachromantischen Zeit* (Heidelberg, 1909).

Goedeke, Karl, *Grundriss zur Geschichte der deutschen Dichtung,* Zweite, ganz neu bearbeitete Auflage, Achtes Buch, siebente Abteilung, Lieferung 2-3 (Berlin, 1955-56), 352-490.

Greeff, Paul, *E. T. A. Hoffmann als Musiker und Musikschriftsteller* (Köln-Krefeld, 1948).

Harich, Walther, *E. T. A. Hoffmann: Das Leben eines Künstlers* (Berlin, n. d. [preface: 1920]).

Hewett-Thayer, Harvey W., *Hoffmann, Author of the Tales* (Princeton, 1948).

Hitzig, Julius Edward, *Aus Hoffmann's Leben und Nachlass,* 2 vols. (Berlin, 1823).

Istel, Edgar, *Die Blütezeit der musikalischen Romantik in Deutschland,* in *Aus Natur und Geisteswelt,* Bd. 239 (Leipzig, 1911).

Jaffé, Aniela, *Bilder und Symbole aus E. T. A. Hoffmanns*

Märchen "Der Goldne Topf," in *Gestaltungen des Un-bewussten*, Bd. VII (Zürich, 1950).

Jennings, Lee B., "Gottfried Keller and the Grotesque," *Monatshefte*, L (1958), 9-20.

Kanzog, Klaus, "Grundzüge der E. T. A.-Hoffmann-Forschung seit 1945," *Mitteilungen der E. T. A. Hoffmann-Gesell-schaft*, 9. Heft (1962), 1-30.

Kayser, Wolfgang, *Das Groteske: Seine Gestaltung in Malerei und Dichtung* (Oldenburg, 1957).

Kron, Wolfgang, *Die angeblichen Freischütz-Kritiken E. T. A. Hoffmanns* (München, 1957).

Martini, Fritz, "Die Märchendichtungen E. T. A. Hoffmanns," *Deutschunterricht*, VII (1955), 56-78.

Mayer, Hans, "Die Wirklichkeit E. T. A. Hoffmanns: Ein Versuch," in E. T. A. Hoffmann, *Poetische Werke* (Berlin, 1958), Vol. I, pp. V-LV.

Mühlher, Robert, "Liebestod und Spiegelmythos in E. T. A. Hoffmanns Märchen 'Der goldne Topf'," in *Dichtung der Krise* (Wien, 1951).

Müller, Hans von, *Die erste Liebe des Ernst Theodor Hoffmann* (Heidelberg, 1955).

——, *Das künstlerische Schaffen E. T. A. Hoffmanns in Umrissen angedeutet* (Leipzig, 1926).

——, "Kurzgefasste Autobibliographie 1896-1929," *Jahresbe-richte der Preussischen Staatsbibliothek*, 1927 f.

——, *Das Kreislerbuch* (Leipzig, 1903).

——, *Lebens-Ansichten des Katers Murr* (Leipzig, 1916).

——, *Nachwort zu E. T. A. Hoffmanns Meister Floh* (Berlin, 1908).

——, (ed.) and Holtze, Friedrich (Einleitungen), *"Das Sanctus" und "Die Brautwahl"* (Berlin, 1910).

Negus, Kenneth, "The Allusions to Schiller's 'Der Geister-seher' in E. T. A. Hoffmann's 'Das Majorat': Meaning and Background," *German Quarterly*, XXXII (1959), 341-355.

——, "E. T. A. Hoffmann's 'Der goldne Topf': Its Romantic Myth," *Germanic Review*, XXXIV (1959), 262-275.

——, "The Family Tree in E. T. A. Hoffmann's 'Die Elixiere des Teufels'," *PMLA*, LXXIII (1958), 516-520.

——, *Thematic Structure in Three Major Works of E. T. A. Hoffmann* (diss. Princeton, 1957), available on microfilm through University Microfilms, Ann Arbor, Michigan.

Neumann, A. R., "Musician or Author? E. T. A. Hoffmann's Decision," *Journal of English and Germanic Philology*, LII (1953), 174-181.

Novalis, *Werke/Briefe. Dokumente*, ed. Ewald Wasmuth (Heidelberg, 1953-1957).

Ochsner, Karl, *E. T. A. Hoffmann als Dichter des Unbewussten* (Frauenfeld/Leipzig, 1936).

Passage, Charles, *Dostoevski the Adapter: A Study in Dostoevski's Use of the Tales of Hoffmann* (Chapel Hill, N.C., 1954).

Pfeiffer-Belli, Wolfgang, "Mythos und Religion bei E. T. A. Hoffmann," *Euphorion*, XXXIV (1933), 305-340.

Planta, Urs Orland von, *E. T. A. Hoffmanns Märchen "Das fremde Kind"* (Bern, 1958).

Ricci, Jean-F.-A, *E. T. A. Hoffmann: L'homme et l'oeuvre* (Paris, 1947).

Schaukal, Richard von, *E. T. A. Hoffmann: Sein Werk aus seinem Leben* (Zürich-Leipzig-Wien, 1923).

Schenck, Ernst von, *E. T. A. Hoffmann: Ein Kampf um das Bild des Menschen* (Berlin, 1939).

Schlegel, A. W., *Vorlesungen über schöne Litteratur und Kunst*, ed. J. Minor, Erster Teil (Heilbronn, 1884).

Schlegel, Friedrich, *Schriften und Fragmente*, ed. E. Behler (Stuttgart, 1956).

——, *Seine prosaischen Jugendschriften*, ed. J. Minor, II (Wien, 1882).

Strich, Fritz, *Die Mythologie in der deutschen Literatur von Klopstock bis Wagner* (Halle a. d. Saale, 1910).

Sucher, Paul, *Les sources du merveilleux chez E. T. A. Hoffmann* (Paris, 1912).

Thalmann, Marianne, "E. T. A. Hoffmanns 'Fräulein von Scuderi'," *Monatshefte*, XLI (1949), 107-116.

———, "E. T. A. Hoffmanns Wirklichkeitsmärchen," *Journal of English and Germanic Philology*, LI (1952), 473-491.

Willimczik, Kurt, *E. T. A. Hoffmann: die drei Reiche seiner Gestaltenwelt* (Berlin, 1939).

Index

Page references in italic figures indicate main discussion